Table of Contents

©2000 by Evan-Moor Corp.

Science Experiments for Young Learners • EMC 866

Earth and Space Science 143

Properties of Earth Materials

Objects in the Sky

Changes in the Earth and Sky

Science and Technology 247

Abilities of Technological Design

Science Experiments for Young Learners

Easy-to-Do Science

- The step-by-step experiments are easy to understand, with illustrations for clarification.
- A materials list is given for each experiment.
- Each experiment includes a student record sheet or an activity sheet and suggestions for logbook activities.
- Each experiment is self-contained. You can decide which experiments support your specific curriculum goals.

Preparation Tips

Before starting any experiment, follow these simple steps:
- Read through the step-by-step directions completely.
- Decide whether the experiment will be done as a teacher demonstration with students assisting, by small groups of students, or by individual students. A few of the experiments (those involving boiling water) must be done by the teacher, with the students observing the results.
- Assemble the materials you will need to conduct the experiment. (The number of sets of materials will vary depending on your grouping decision.)
- Reproduce the record sheet for the experiment.

Helpful Hints

Plan ahead to keep the "mess" to a minimum.
- Arrange materials and equipment on a science supply table.
- When using water, work on a tray or over a shallow plastic tub to catch spills and overflows. Have towels ready for emergencies.
- Explain set-up and clean-up procedures carefully each time you do an experiment.
- Emphasize safety.

Science Experiments for Young Learners • EMC 866

Science Experiments and Logbooks

As you do the experiments in this book, you may want to keep a science logbook. Logbooks are valuable learning tools for several reasons:

- Logbooks give students an opportunity to put what they are learning into their own words.

- Putting ideas into words is an important step in internalizing new information. Whether spoken or written, this experience allows students to synthesize their thinking.

- Explaining and describing experiences helps students make connections between several concepts and ideas.

- Logbook entries allow the teacher to catch misunderstandings right away and then reteach.

- Logbooks are a useful reference for students and a record of what has been learned.

Using a Logbook

Two types of logbook pages are provided in this resource book.

Record and activity sheets for individual experiments

Most experiments have special record sheets that allow beginning writers and readers to respond to the experiments and to log their observations easily. Other experiments have related activity sheets. Collect these pages as they are completed and compile them to create a science logbook for each student.

Open-ended logbook pages

At the end of each section is a form that can be used to respond to any experiment in that section. Use these forms when no record sheet is provided for an experiment or when you want to encourage a more detailed response to an experiment.

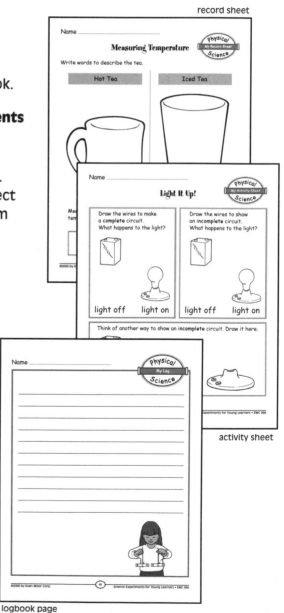

record sheet

activity sheet

logbook page

Science Experiments for Young Learners • EMC 866

Physical Science

- Objects have observable properties.

- Properties are measured using tools.

- Objects are made of one or more materials.

- Materials can exist in different states.

- The position and motion of objects can be changed by pushing and pulling.

- Sound is produced by vibrating objects.

- Light travels in a straight line.

Science Experiments for Young Learners • EMC 866

What Is It?

Properties of Objects and Materials

Objects have observable properties.
Students confirm that certain identifying properties of an object can be felt.

Doing the Experiment

1. Divide students into groups of two or three.

2. Give each team a brown paper lunch bag containing a familiar object.

3. Each team member reaches into the bag without looking and feels the object in the bag. The feeler thinks of a word that describes the object.

4. Teams choose three words that tell about the object without naming it (*metal, flat, smooth, cold, hard*).

5. The words are written on the bag tag. The bag tag is stapled to the top of the bag with the object still inside.

Sharing the Results

Teams read the words on their bag tags. The class tries to guess the object in the bag.

Making Connections

Bring a box with a label that describes the contents. Read the description. Ask students, "Have you ever seen a label on a box or bag that describes the thing inside? Why would it be important to know the description?"

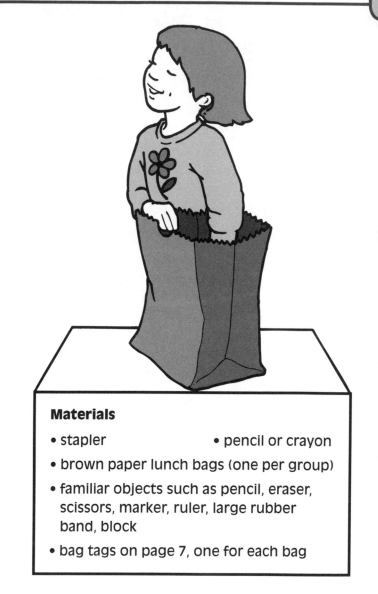

Materials

- stapler
- pencil or crayon
- brown paper lunch bags (one per group)
- familiar objects such as pencil, eraser, scissors, marker, ruler, large rubber band, block
- bag tags on page 7, one for each bag

Science Experiments for Young Learners • EMC 866

Properties of This Object:

_____

_____

_____

Properties of This Object:

_____

_____

_____

Properties of This Object:

_____

_____

_____

 Science Experiments for Young Learners • EMC 866

Bend It!

Properties of Objects and Materials

Objects have observable properties.
Students test common items and sort them into "bend" and "don't bend" groups.

Doing the Experiment

1. Divide your students into small groups.

2. Give each group a bag containing 8 to 10 objects from your materials collection and a copy of the sorting mat.

3. Students take an object from the bag and predict whether it will bend.

4. Students test the object to see if it bends. Objects in the bags should be sorted into two groups—those that bend and those that do not bend.

5. Students can tape the objects to the sorting mat or draw and label the objects in the correct areas.

Sharing the Results

Have students report the results of their experiment. Record the materials that bend on a large chart or on the chalkboard.

Making Connections

Ask students to find other objects in the classroom that bend. Ask students, "Why it is important for some materials to bend? What things do you use every day that bend? Is it important that some things don't bend? What things?"

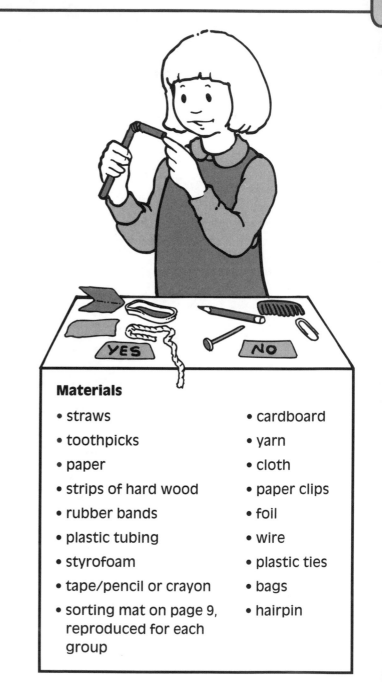

Materials

- straws
- toothpicks
- paper
- strips of hard wood
- rubber bands
- plastic tubing
- styrofoam
- tape/pencil or crayon
- sorting mat on page 9, reproduced for each group
- cardboard
- yarn
- cloth
- paper clips
- foil
- wire
- plastic ties
- bags
- hairpin

Name _____

Will It Bend?

Yes	No

Science Experiments for Young Learners • EMC 866

Soak It Up!

Properties of Objects and Materials

Objects have observable properties.

Students test common items to find out which ones absorb water.

Doing the Experiment

1. Divide your students into small groups.

2. Give each group a bag containing 8 to 10 objects from your materials collection, a container of water, an eyedropper, and a copy of the sorting mat.

3. Students take an object from the bag and predict whether it will absorb the water.

4. Students test the object by dropping three drops of water on it and waiting five counts. Objects in the bags should be sorted into two groups—those that absorb and those that do not absorb.

5. Students can tape the objects to the sorting mat or draw or write the names of the objects in the correct areas.

Sharing the Results

Have students report the results of their experiment. Record the materials that absorb water on a large chart or the chalkboard.

Making Connections

Ask students to find other objects in the classroom that absorb. Ask, "Why it is important for some materials to absorb? What things do you use every day that absorb? Is it important that some things don't absorb? What things?"

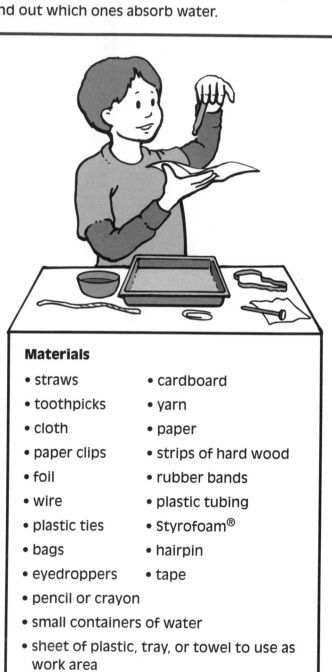

Materials

- straws
- toothpicks
- cloth
- paper clips
- foil
- wire
- plastic ties
- bags
- eyedroppers
- pencil or crayon
- cardboard
- yarn
- paper
- strips of hard wood
- rubber bands
- plastic tubing
- Styrofoam®
- hairpin
- tape
- small containers of water
- sheet of plastic, tray, or towel to use as work area
- sorting mat on page 11, reproduced for each group

Science Experiments for Young Learners • EMC 866

Will It Absorb?

Yes

No

Just Passing Through

Properties of Objects and Materials

Objects have observable properties.

Students sort objects into groups according to the amount of light that passes through the materials.

Doing the Experiment

1. Show three cups—one clear glass, one colored plastic, and one Styrofoam®. Fill the glasses with the same liquid. Ask students to tell what is in each glass. Ask, "Is it easier to tell what is in one glass? Why?" Students should observe that if you can see through a material (glass) it is easier to tell what is in the glass.

2. Show students an assortment of materials. (See materials list.) Students will judge whether they can see through each material. Set up a procedure for this:

   • Students hold the object up to a light source.

   • Students sort the materials into three categories:

     a lot of light passes through

     a little light passes through

     no light passes through

Sharing the Results

Have students share their observations. Depending on the level of your students, you may want to introduce the terms *transparent* to describe materials that let a lot of light pass through, *translucent* for materials that let a little light pass through, and *opaque* for materials that let no light pass through.

Making Connections

Have students look for materials at home that fit the three categories. Give them the record sheet and have them record their findings. When record sheets are returned, compile a class list of items in the three categories.

Materials

- one clear glass cup
- one colored plastic cup
- one Styrofoam® cup
- cardboard
- aluminum foil
- wood
- clear acetate
- light source (e.g., flashlight, lamp)
- record sheet on page 13, reproduced for individual students
- towel
- plastic bowl
- ceramic tile
- cellophane
- tissue paper
- muslin
- waxed paper

Science Experiments for Young Learners • EMC 866

Name _____

Just Passing Through

I found these materials at home.

a lot of light passes through

a little light passes through

no light passes through

Science Experiments for Young Learners • EMC 866

Measuring Temperature

Properties of Objects and Materials

Properties are measured using tools.

Students confirm that temperature is a property that can be measured using a thermometer.

Doing the Experiment

1. Describe the two containers of tea. Tell how they are alike and how they are different. Record the responses on a class chart and on individual record pages. *(Both containers hold tea. Because the shapes of the containers are different, the shape of the liquid is different. The cup is hot. The glass is cold.)*

2. Confirm that one of the properties of the two liquids is their temperature. Ask students, "How can we measure the temperature?"

3. Demonstrate the use of a thermometer.

4. Measure the temperature of the two containers of tea.

Sharing the Results

Record the temperatures on a class chart and on the record sheets. Discuss why it might be important to document the temperature of something.

Materials

- 2 thermometers
- a glass of iced tea
- a cup of hot tea
- record sheet on page 15, reproduced for individual students

Making Connections

A weatherperson often gives the temperature as part of a weather report. Ask, "Why is it important that the air temperature be measured? What other things do we measure the temperature of?"

Science Experiments for Young Learners • EMC 866

Name _____

Measuring Temperature

Write words to describe the tea.

| Hot Tea | Iced Tea |

Measure and record the temperature.

Measure and record the temperature.

Science Experiments for Young Learners • EMC 866

How Heavy?

Properties of Objects and Materials

Properties are measured using tools.

Students compare the weight of two items using nonstandard units of measurement.

Doing the Experiment

1. Describe the two fruits. Record the descriptions on a class chart and on the individual record sheet. If weight is not one of the descriptors, ask, "Which fruit is heavier?"

2. Have students make predictions about which is heavier and then discuss ways to test the predictions.

3. Use the balance to compare the weight. Note which fruit is heavier. Then ask, "How can we measure how much heavier it is?"

4. Weigh each of the fruits using several nontraditional measures.

   For example, "The apple weighs 24 counting bears. The orange weighs 30 counting bears."

   "The apple weighs 4 blocks. The orange weighs 5 blocks."

Materials

- an apple
- a balance
- an orange
- an assortment of possible units of measure—counting bears, small wooden blocks, packing peanuts, metal washers, beans, etc.
- record sheet on page 17, reproduced for individual students

Sharing the Results

Answer the question "How much heavier?" (In the examples, the orange is 6 counting bears heavier than the apple. The orange is 1 block heavier than the apple.) Record the answer.

Making Connections

Ask, "When would it be important to measure weight?"

Science Experiments for Young Learners • EMC 866

Name _____

How Heavy?

Write words to tell about the two fruits.

How heavy is the apple?

[ ]

How heavy is the orange?

[ ]

Which is heavy?

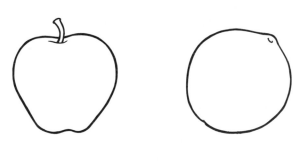

How much heavier?

[ ]

Science Experiments for Young Learners • EMC 866

How Heavy?

Properties of Objects and Materials

Properties are measured using tools.

Students compare the weight of two items using standard units of measurement.

Doing the Experiment

1. Describe the two fruits. Record the descriptions on a class chart and on the record sheet. If weight is not one of the descriptors, ask, "Which fruit is heavier?"

2. Have students make predictions about which is heavier and then discuss ways to test the predictions.

3. Use the balance to compare the weight. Note which is heavier. Then ask, "How can we tell how much heavier it is?"

4. Weigh each of the fruits using traditional weights. Record the weights on the record sheet.

Sharing the Results

Answer the question "How much heavier?" Record which fruit is heavier on the record sheets. Ask, "Why would it be important to measure with a standard measure?"

Making Connections

Ask, "What other things have you weighed? Was it important that the weights be standard? Why?"

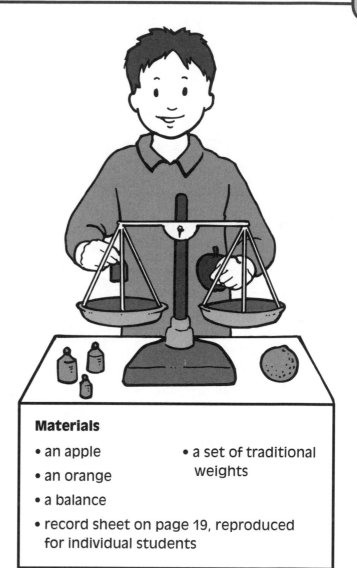

Materials

- an apple
- an orange
- a balance
- record sheet on page 19, reproduced for individual students
- a set of traditional weights

Name _____

How Heavy?

Write words to tell about the two fruits.

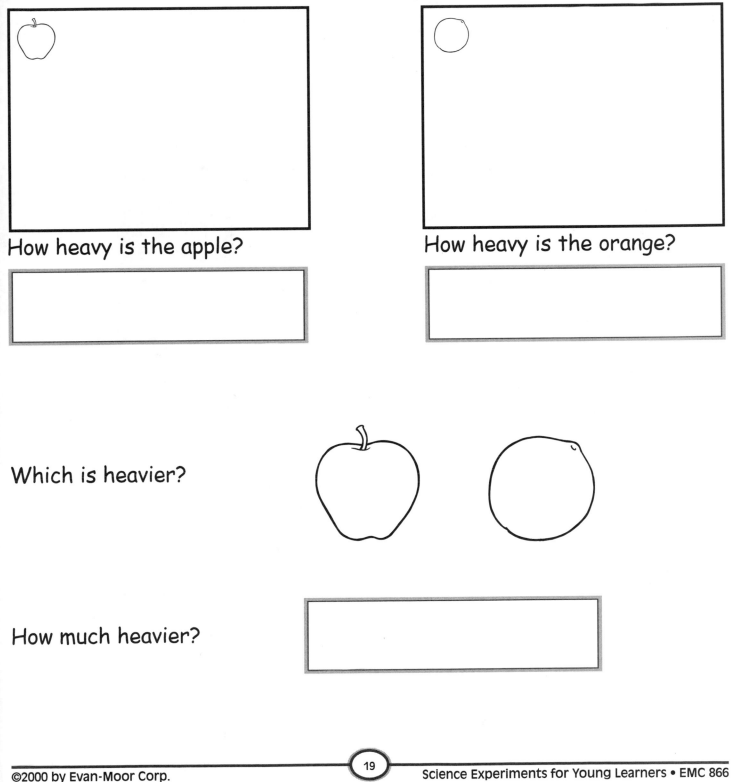

How heavy is the apple?

How heavy is the orange?

Which is heavier?

How much heavier?

Science Experiments for Young Learners • EMC 866

How Long?

Properties of Objects and Materials

Properties are measured using tools.

Students compare the height, length, and width of common classroom items using nonstandard units of measurement.

Doing the Experiment

1. Each student chooses a familiar classroom object.

2. Students draw their objects on their record sheets.

3. Students measure the height, length, and width of their objects using a nonstandard unit of measure of their choice.

4. Students record the measurements on the record sheets.

Sharing the Results

Have students share their record sheets. Then do some comparing.

- Point out a comparison where the smaller object has a larger number of units.

   For example, "Tommy's desk is 6 cards long. The table is 4 blocks long. Which is longer?"

- After students answer, point out the discrepancy.

   "The desk is 6 and the table is 4, but the table is longer. That doesn't seem right. What is the problem?"

- Ask, "How could we solve the problem of different-sized units?"

Making Connections

Create a list of things that one might have a reason to measure.

Materials

- classroom objects—desks, tables, bookshelves, chalkboards, easels

- an assortment of possible units of measure—paper clips, counters, dominoes, index cards, Unifix® cubes, blocks, pencils, scarves, pointers, etc.

- record sheet on page 21, reproduced for individual students

Science Experiments for Young Learners • EMC 866

Name _____

How Long?

Draw the thing you will measure.
What will you use to measure it? _____

┌─────────────────────────────────────┐
│   │
│   │
│   │
│   │
│   │
│   │
│   │
│   │
└─────────────────────────────────────┘

Record the measurements.

It is _____ long.

It is _____ wide.

It is _____ tall.

Science Experiments for Young Learners • EMC 866

How Long?

Properties of Objects and Materials

Properties are measured using tools.

Students compare the height, length, and width of common classroom items using standard units of measurement.

Doing the Experiment

Note: Demonstrate the use of a ruler if your students are unfamiliar with measuring.

1. Each student chooses a familiar classroom object.

2. Students draw their objects on their record sheets.

3. Students measure the height and length of their objects using rulers.

4. Students record the measurement.

Sharing the Results

Have students share their record sheets. Then do some comparing.

- Point out a comparison. For example, "The desk is 2 feet long. The table is 4 feet long."

- Ask, "Is it easier to compare things if we all use the same unit of measure?"

Making Connections

Ask, "Why is it important for people all around the world to use a standard unit of measurement?"

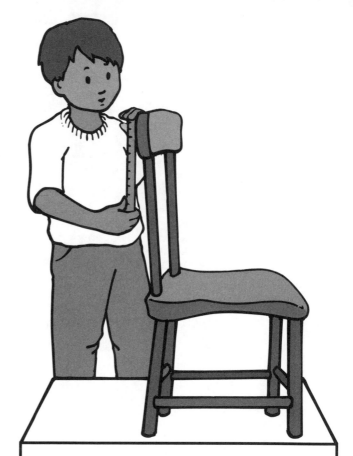

Materials

- classroom objects—desks, bookshelves, tables, chalkboards, easels

- rulers

- record sheet on page 23, reproduced for individual students

Name _____

How Long?

Draw the thing you will measure.
What will you use to measure it? _____

Record the measurements.

It is _____ long.

It is _____ wide.

It is _____ tall.

Plates, Plates, Plates

Properties of Objects and Materials

Objects are made of one or more materials.
Students sort common objects into groups made from the same material.

Doing the Experiment

1. Show the collection of plates. Ask, "What is the plate made of?"

2. Label the plates with the prepared labels.

3. Students choose an object from the collection of objects and put it on the plate made from the same material.

Sharing the Results

Record the objects in each plate on a large chart. Ask students to describe how all the objects of one material are alike.

Making Connections

Students choose classroom items to add to the plates. Ask, "Are there some objects in the classroom that could go onto more than one plate? Are there some objects that don't go on any plate?"

Materials

- a collection of plates: a paper plate, a metal pie pan, a glass pie pan, a shallow wooden tray or bowl, and a plastic plate

- a collection of objects: straws, wooden blocks, plastic building blocks, small cardboard boxes, wooden building sticks, wire, toothpicks, washers, paper clips, cups, tongue depressors, craft sticks, paper cups, coffee stirrers, paper, nuts and bolts, coat hangers, foil, newspaper, juice cans, screws

- labels for the plates on page 25

Science Experiments for Young Learners • EMC 866

Plate Labels

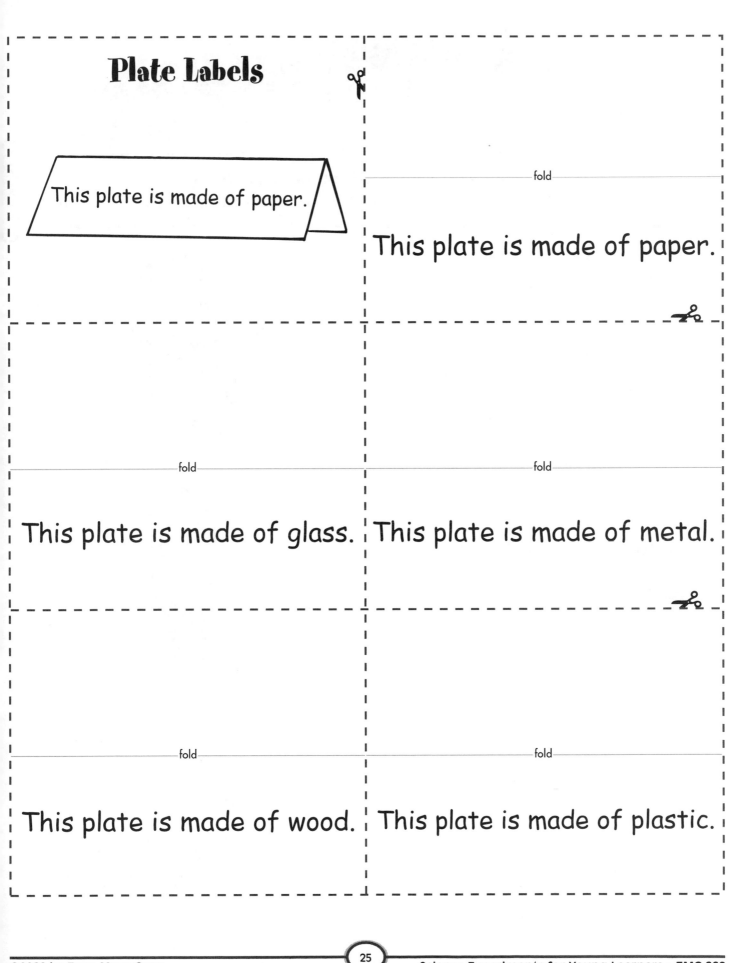

This plate is made of paper.

This plate is made of paper.

This plate is made of glass.

This plate is made of metal.

This plate is made of wood.

This plate is made of plastic.

fold

fold

fold

fold

fold

Science Experiments for Young Learners • EMC 866

I Spy

Properties of Objects and Materials

Objects are made of one or more materials.

Students identify an object in their surroundings after being told what material(s) it is made from.

Doing the Experiment

1. Students follow the directions to make spy-scopes.

2. Model the activity.

   • Look through your scope.

   • Focus on one object. Think of what material that object is made of.

   • Say "I spy something made of <u>(name of a material)</u>."

3. Students look through their scopes, pointing them in the same direction as yours. They guess what you are looking at.

4. Repeat the activity with new "spyers."

Sharing the Results

As the objects are guessed, have students check to confirm that the objects are really made of the named material(s).

Making Connections

Ask students why an object is made of a particular material. For example, "Why are the curtains made of cloth?"

Cloth can bend when the curtains are pulled.

It keeps the room quieter.

It looks pretty.

It can be cut in different lengths and sewn on a sewing machine.

Materials

• classroom
• tape
• spy-scope pattern on page 27, reproduced for individual students
• crayons

Spy-Scope Pattern

1. Color   2. Cut   3. Paste   4. Look!

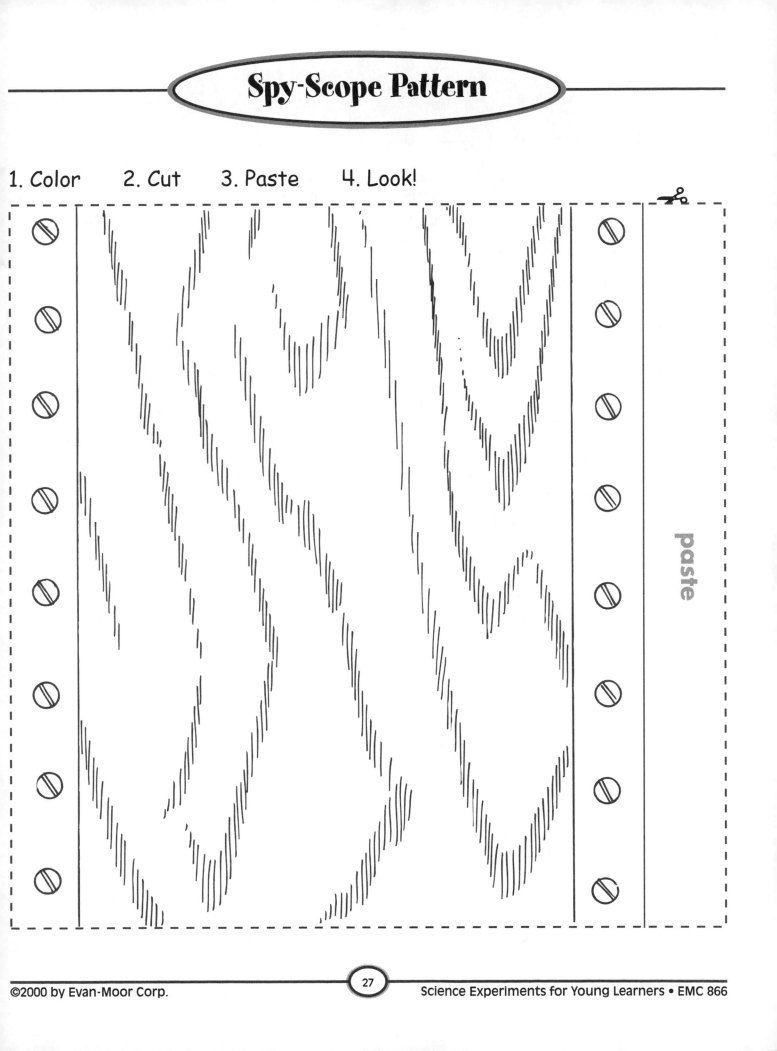

paste

Science Experiments for Young Learners • EMC 866

Make a Material Book

Properties of Objects and Materials

Objects are made of one or more materials.

Students use small objects or magazine pictures of items, identify the material(s) from which each is made, and paste each object or picture on the appropriate page of a class book.

Doing the Experiment

1. Label a posterboard page with the name of a material.

2. Have students choose an object or picture of an object that is made of that material.

3. Glue the objects and pictures to the posterboard page.

4. Label each object with the student's words (e.g., *"This wagon is made of metal. I have one just like it at home."*).

5. Repeat these steps using additional posters for other materials.

Sharing the Results

Read the class materials book together.

Making Connections

Students go on a materials hunt at home. They draw or glue the materials they find in their own materials books.

Materials

- glue
- hole punch
- yarn
- marking pen
- small objects or magazine pictures
- posterboard sheet for each material to be included in the book: plastic, paper, wood, metal, glass, and paper
- book of materials on page 29, reproduced for individual students

Science Experiments for Young Learners • EMC 866

Name

My Little Book
of Materials

2

This is made of plastic.

3

This is made of wood.

4

This is made of metal.

5

This is made of glass.

6

This is made of paper.

What's in the Bowl?

Properties of Objects and Materials

Materials can exist in different states.

Students learn that the same material (in this case water and glue) can exist as a liquid and as a solid.

Doing the Experiment

1. Show the bowls of materials. Make sure that students know what is in each bowl.

2. Have students sort the bowls into liquids and solids.

Sharing the Results

Ask, "What is the same about the ice and the water? What is the same about the liquid glue and the solid glue? What does this tell us about materials?" *(The same material can exist as a liquid and as a solid.)* Students complete their record sheets.

Making Connections

Make butter (solid) from cream (liquid). Pour cream into a plastic container with a lid. Shake until butter forms.

Materials

• 4 identical clear bowls
• small amounts of:
  ice
  water
  liquid white glue
  hardened white glue

• record sheet on page 31, reproduced for individual students

Science Experiments for Young Learners • EMC 866

Name _____

What's in the Bowl?

Cut and paste to put the liquids together and the solids together.
Draw a line between the things that are made of the same materials.

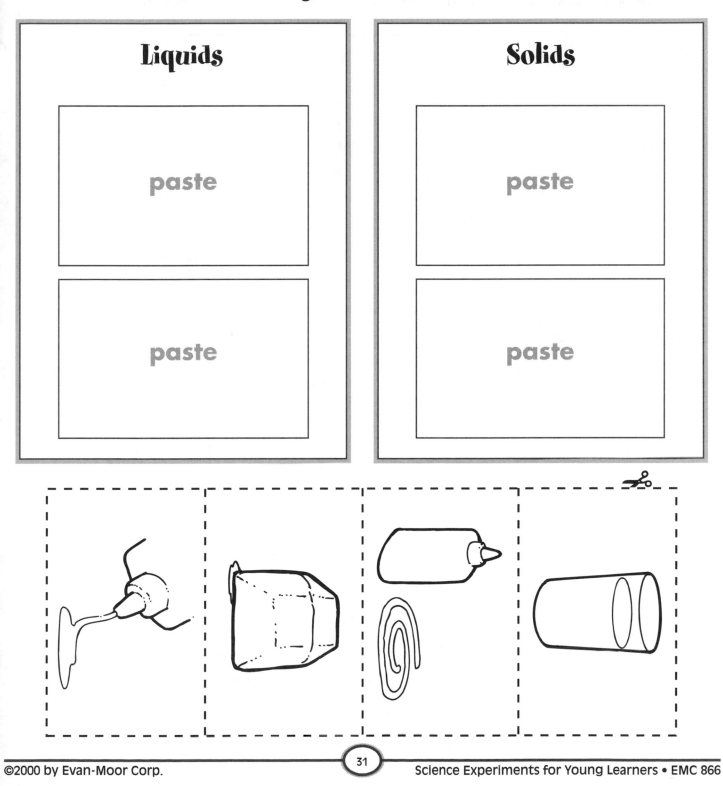

Liquids

paste

paste

Solids

paste

paste

Science Experiments for Young Learners • EMC 866

Strange Stuff

Properties of Objects and Materials

Materials can exist in different states.

Students find out that mixing materials together can result in a new material with very different properties.

Doing the Experiment

1. Ask students to describe the cornstarch and the water. Write their observations on a chart or chalkboard.

2. Students predict how the materials will change when they are combined, then record their predictions.

3. Students combine the cornstarch and the water.

4. Students explore ways that the new "stuff" behaves.

   • They roll the mixture in their hands.

   • They open their hands to let it run off onto the saucer.

   • They stir the mixture and try to scoop it up with the spoon.

5. Students describe how the cornstarch and the water have changed, then record their observations as they fill in their record sheets.

Sharing the Results

Using the information on the charts and individual record sheets, write a description of the mixture.

(For example, "Strange Stuff is cool. It makes a ball in my hand, so it is a solid. Then it melts back onto the saucer, so it is a liquid. It feels soft and smooth.")

Making Connections

Ask students if they have ever combined two things that formed a new material. Suggest cooking experiences if your students seem stumped.

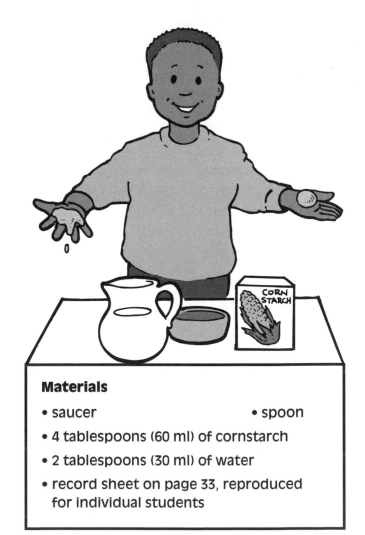

Materials

• saucer   • spoon

• 4 tablespoons (60 ml) of cornstarch

• 2 tablespoons (30 ml) of water

• record sheet on page 33, reproduced for individual students

Science Experiments for Young Learners • EMC 866

Name _____

Strange Stuff

Draw and write to show what happened.

What I started with

What I think will happen

What happened

Science Experiments for Young Learners • EMC 866

Watch It Melt!

Properties of Objects and Materials

Materials can exist in different states.
Students learn that some materials can be both a solid and a liquid.

Doing the Experiment

1. Put an ice cube on the plastic plate.

2. Put the plate in a warm place.

3. Watch to see what will happen.

4. Cut and paste to show what happened.

Sharing the Results

Students share their observations.
Ask students to infer why the ice melted.

Making Connections

Ask students, "Do all solids melt?" Look at a popsicle, a pebble, and a crayon. Have students predict which will melt. Leave the three items in a hot place and test the predictions.

Have students suggest other solids that will melt *(butter, chocolate, ice cream)*.

Materials

- plastic plates
- ice cubes
- popsicle
- pebble
- crayon
- record sheet on page 35, reproduced for individual students

Science Experiments for Young Learners • EMC 866

Name _____

Watch It Melt!

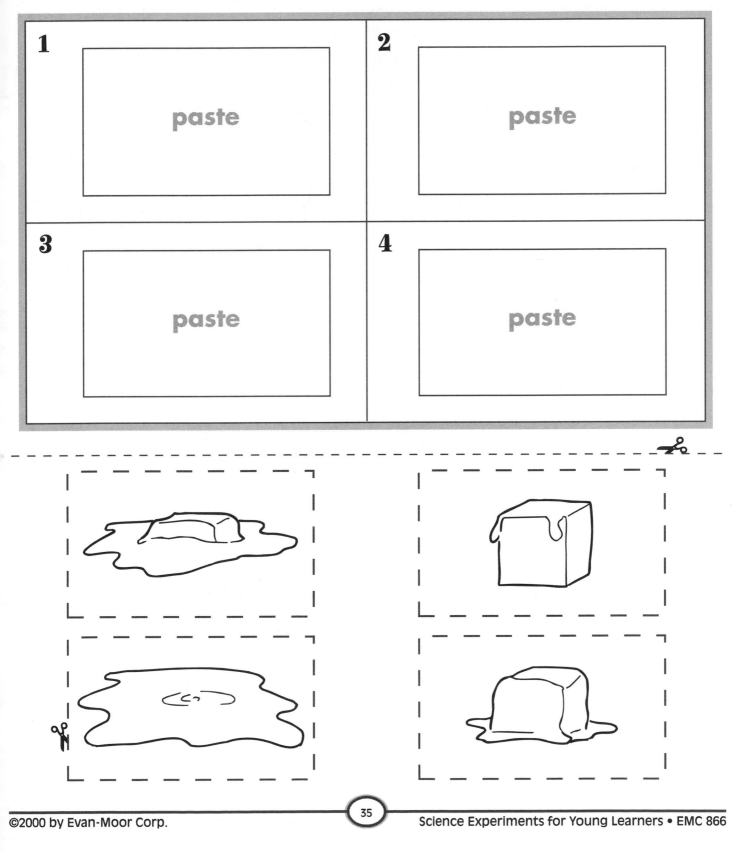

1   paste

2   paste

3   paste

4   paste

Science Experiments for Young Learners • EMC 866

Disappearing Water

Properties of Objects and Materials

Materials can exist in different states.
Students learn that water can evaporate and become a gas.

Doing the Experiment

1. Students write their names on the plastic glasses with the marking pen.

2. Fill the glasses about half full of water.

3. Mark the water level on each glass with the marking pen.

4. Color the first glass on the record sheet to match.

5. Set the glasses in a warm place. Students predict what they think will happen to the water in the glasses.

6. Wait three days. Check the glasses. Mark the new water level on the glass and record the change on the record sheet.

Sharing the Results

Ask students to describe the change they observed. Ask, "Did the water change? Where do you think the water went?" Confirm with as detailed an explanation of *evaporation* as is appropriate for the age and ability of your students. Students should mark the picture at the bottom of their record sheet that answers the question.

Making Connections

Ask "Can you think of other places water could evaporate?" *(rivers, oceans, puddles, fishbowls, swimming pools)*

Materials

- clear plastic glasses
- permanent marking pens
- record sheet on page 37, reproduced for individual students
- water
- blue crayons

Science Experiments for Young Learners • EMC 866

Name _____

Disappearing Water

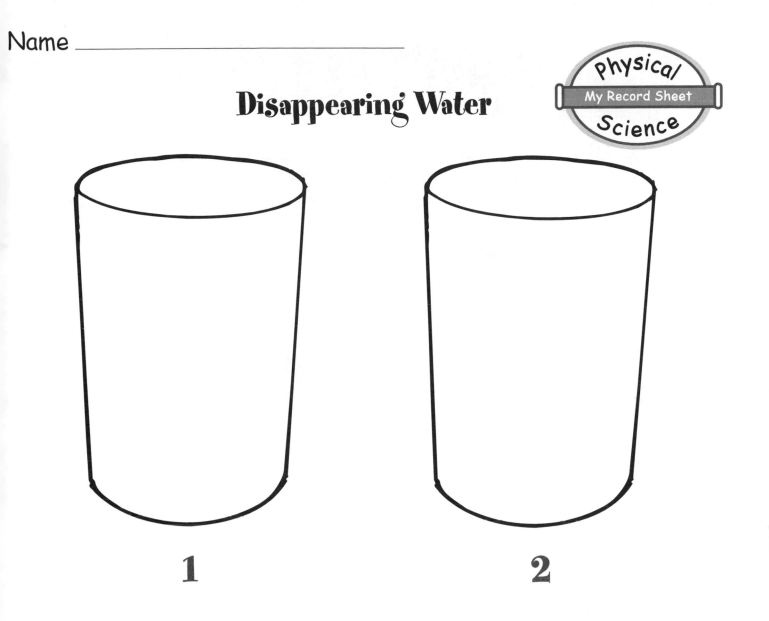

1   2

What happened to the water?

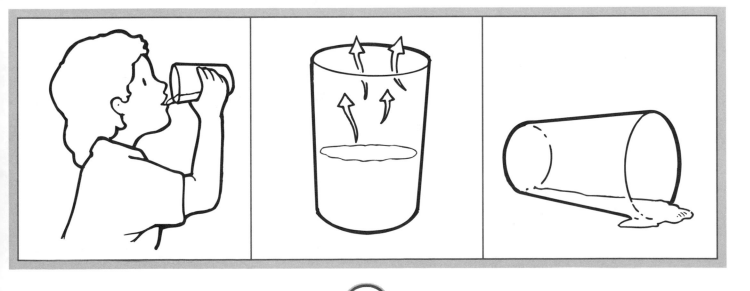

Science Experiments for Young Learners • EMC 866

Ice Cube on a String

Properties of Objects and Materials

Materials can exist in different states.

Students perform what seems to be a trick to learn that water can change from solid to liquid and vice versa.

Doing the Experiment

1. Soak the thread in water and lay it on top of the ice cube.

2. Sprinkle a little salt all along the part of the thread that is touching the cube.

3. Wait about 30 seconds.

4. Lift the thread.

Sharing the Results

Have students explain what they think happened to make this "trick" work. Confirm perceptions that are correct. Correct misconceptions. Then have students complete their record sheets.

The salt melts the ice where the thread lies. The cold ice freezes the water again and traps the thread in the ice cube.

Making Connections

A snowy or icy road is dangerous because it is very slippery. Putting salt on the road turns the ice or snow to water. Ask, "What would happen if very cold air then touched the water?"

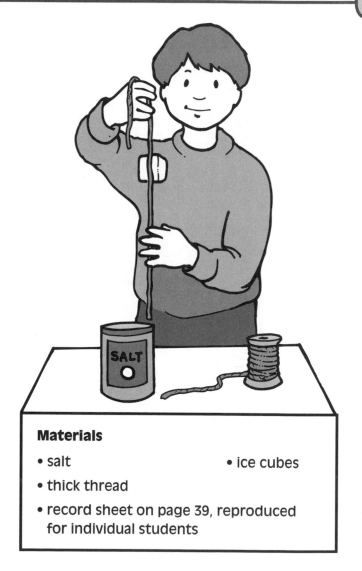

Materials

- salt
- thick thread
- ice cubes
- record sheet on page 39, reproduced for individual students

Science Experiments for Young Learners • EMC 866

Name _____

Lifting an Ice Cube

Cut and paste to tell what happened.

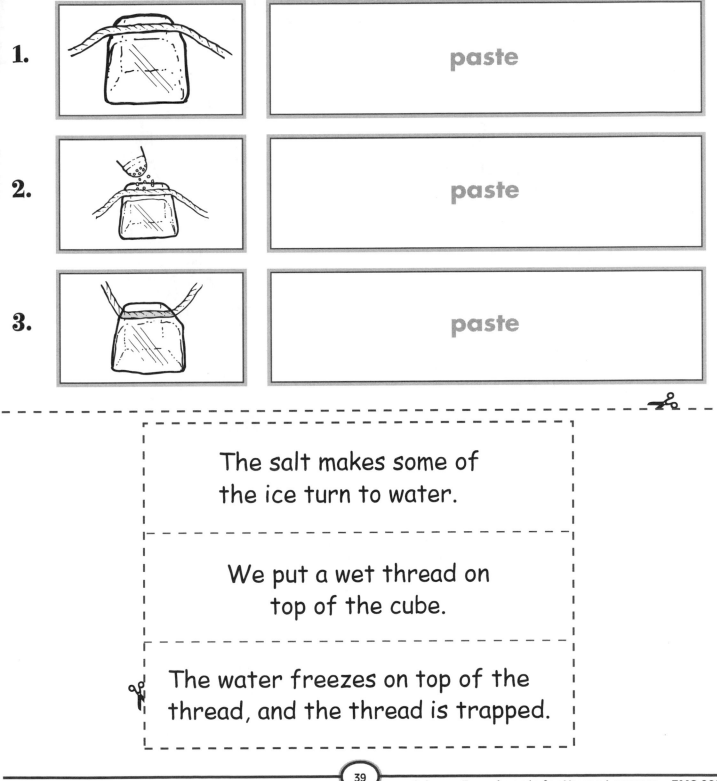

1. | paste

2. | paste

3. | paste

The salt makes some of
the ice turn to water.

We put a wet thread on
top of the cube.

The water freezes on top of the
thread, and the thread is trapped.

Water in the Air

Properties of Objects and Materials

Materials can exist in different states.
Students observe that water vapor condenses out of the air when air strikes a cold surface.

Doing the Experiment

1. Put several ice cubes in the jar.

2. Put the lid on the jar and wipe off the outside of the jar with a paper towel.

3. Let the jar sit in a warm place for a little while. Look at the jar to see what has happened.

4. Record the observation on the record sheet by circling the jar that shows what happened.

Sharing the Results

Ask students, "What did you find on the outside of your jar? Where did the water come from?" You may want to explain to your students that when the warm air touches the cold jar, the water in the air forms into drops they can see (condensation).

Making Connections

Ask students, "Can you think of another place where you have seen water that came from the air?" *(windshield, pitcher of lemonade, dew on the grass)*

Materials

- ice cubes
- paper towels
- jars with lids (Note: You can use clear plastic cups covered with plastic wrap held in place with rubber bands.)
- record sheet on page 41, reproduced for individual students

Science Experiments for Young Learners • EMC 866

Name _____

Water in the Air

Science Experiments for Young Learners • EMC 866

A Melting Race

Materials can exist in different states.

Students experiment to see if the size of ice pieces affects the melting rate.

Doing the Experiment

1. Put water in two glasses.

2. Put a large ice cube in one glass and several small pieces of ice in the other.

3. Ask students to predict which ice will melt faster.

4. Observe what happens.

5. Record the results on the record sheet.

Sharing the Results

Ask, "Did the little pieces of ice melt faster or slower than the large ice cube? Why do you think that happened?"

The more surface area of a solid that is exposed to heat, the faster the solid will melt.

Making Connections

Ask, "If you wanted to keep your soft drink cold for a long time, should you use ice cubes or crushed ice? Why would you use a block of ice instead of ice cubes in a punch bowl?"

Materials

- plastic glasses
- large ice cubes
- water
- small pieces of ice
- record sheet on page 43, reproduced for individual students

Name _____

A Melting Race

Push and Pull

Position and Motion of Objects

The position and motion of objects can be changed by pushing or pulling.
Students demonstrate that a swing can be moved by pushing or pulling.

Doing the Experiment

Have students show different ways they can make the swing move.

Sharing the Results

Ask, "Did the swing move by itself?" Help students understand that the swing is not able to move by itself.

Introduce the two terms *pushing* and *pulling*. Ask students to categorize the swing movements on the record sheet.

The swing is a pendulum. A push or a pull gives the swing enough energy to put it into action. Isaac Newton stated this principle—An object at rest will remain at rest unless a force acts upon it.

Making Connections

Ask students to think of other things they move by pushing or pulling. Make a list of the objects named.

Materials

- a swing
- individual students
- record sheet on page 45, reproduced for individual students

---

Science Experiments for Young Learners • EMC 866

Name _____

Push and Pull

I can make the swing move in two different ways.

This is a push.

This is a pull.

This is a push.

This is a pull.

Science Experiments for Young Learners • EMC 866

Marshmallow Launch

Position and Motion of Objects

The position and motion of objects can be changed by pushing or pulling.
Students use a catapult to "push" marshmallows.

Doing the Experiment

1. Show the materials. Accept suggestions on how to use them to move a marshmallow.

2. Follow these steps to build a catapult to launch the marshmallows.

   • Tape a plastic spoon to a wooden block.

   • Attach the block and the spoon to a wooden ruler, using the rubber band.

3. Show students how to launch a marshmallow by placing it in the spoon and carefully pulling the spoon back and releasing it.

4. Make a circle on the floor with yarn. Have students launch marshmallows into the circle.

Sharing the Results

Students share marshmallow-launching experiences. Ask them to explain what caused the marshmallow to move. Encourage them to explain how they changed the distance that the marshmallows went.

Students complete the record sheet to show how they moved the marshmallows.

Making Connections

Talk about a gymnast jumping on a small trampoline and then vaulting. Ask, "How is the gymnast like the marshmallow?"

Materials
• miniature marshmallows   • yarn
• for each catapult:
   rubber band
   plastic spoon
   wooden block
   wooden ruler
   masking tape
• record sheet on page 47, reproduced for individual students

Science Experiments for Young Learners • EMC 866

Name _____

Moving a Marshmallow

Draw the catapult.
Show the path of the marshmallow.

The marshmallow moved because it was **pushed**   **pulled**   .

Science Experiments for Young Learners • EMC 866

Going on a Motion Hunt

Position and Motion of Objects

The position and motion of objects can be changed by pushing or pulling.
Students find common objects that can be moved by pushing or pulling.

Doing the Experiment

1. Look around a defined area.

2. Students point out objects that are moved by pushing or pulling.

3. Draw or list the objects on the class chart.

4. Give students individual record sheets and have them move to a new area and record the objects they see there.

Sharing the Results

Students share the observations on their record sheets.

Making Connections

Create sentence strips.

I can push a _____ .
I can pull a _____ .

Help students read the phrases, copy and complete the sentences correctly, and then illustrate the sentences.

Materials

- class chart
- record sheet on page 49, reproduced for individual students

Science Experiments for Young Learners • EMC 866

Name _____

A Motion Hunt

Things That Are Pushed	Things That Are Pulled

Science Experiments for Young Learners • EMC 866

Twisting and Turning

Position and Motion of Objects

The position and motion of objects can be changed by pushing or pulling.
Students learn that gravity can move objects by pulling on them.

Doing the Experiment

1. Cut, color, and fold the spinners.

2. Put a paper clip on the end of each spinner to hold the folds in place.

3. Drop the spinners. (You may want to have students stand on a table or chair, or take them outside and drop the spinners from the platform on a slide or from a climbing apparatus. Make sure that an adult is on duty as a spotter.)

4. Ask, "How do the spinners move?"

Sharing the Results

Have students describe the spinners' flights. Record words that describe the movement. (You may want to introduce the idea that the force of gravity pulled the spinner to the ground. If you are outside, moving air may push the spinners as well.)

Making Connections

Ask, "What other things are pulled to the ground in a similar way?" If possible, find some maple seedpods to share with your class.

Materials
- scissors
- crayons
- paper clips
- spinner pattern on page 51, reproduced for individual students

Science Experiments for Young Learners • EMC 866

Spinner Pattern

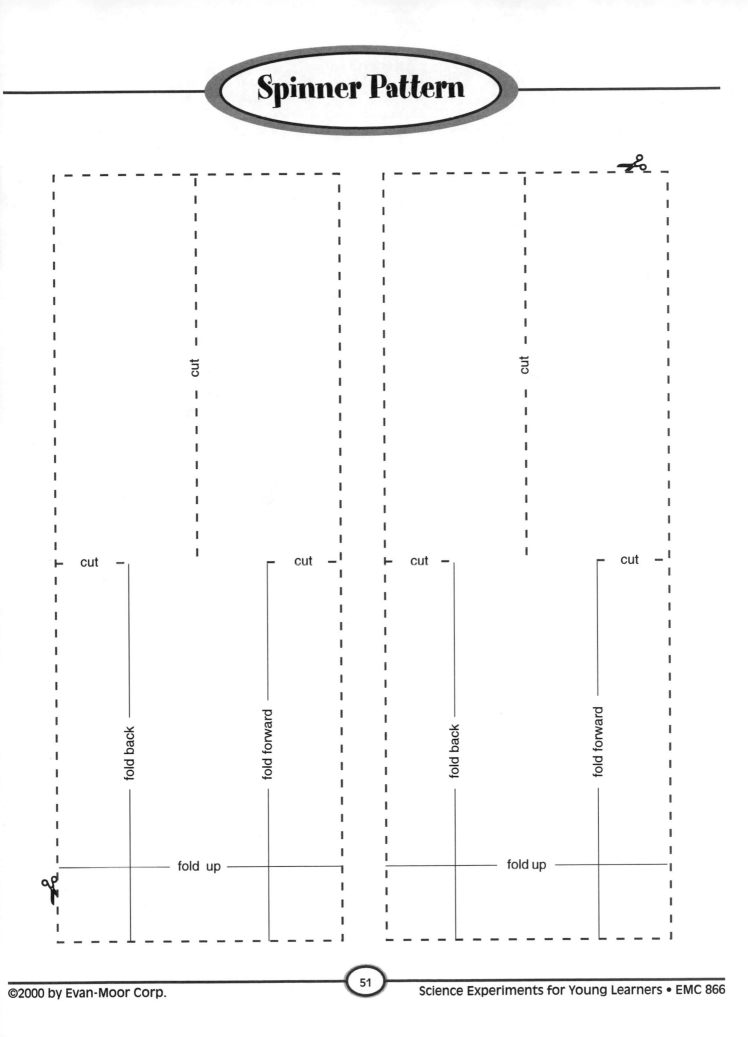

Science Experiments for Young Learners • EMC 866

Playing a Rubber Band Ukulele

Position and Motion of Objects

Sound is produced by vibrating objects.
Students make sound by vibrating a rubber band.

Doing the Experiment

1. Students make rubber band ukuleles.

   • Wrap a rubber band around the two ends of a ruler.

   • Push a pencil underneath the rubber band.

2. Students play the ukuleles.

   • Pluck the rubber band.

   • Move the pencil and pluck again.

Sharing the Results

Have students share observations about the sounds they made with their ukuleles. Guide students to recognize that the sounds were made when plucking the rubber band, causing it to move back and forth (vibrate). The sound is higher or lower depending on the placement of the pencil.

Making Connections

Ask, "What musical instruments make sounds in a way similar to the rubber band ukulele?"

Materials
• rubber bands

• rulers

• pencils

• record sheet on page 53, reproduced for individual students

Science Experiments for Young Learners • EMC 866

Name _____

Playing a
Rubber Band Ukulele

Draw the pencil to show its position.
Mark whether the sound was low or high.

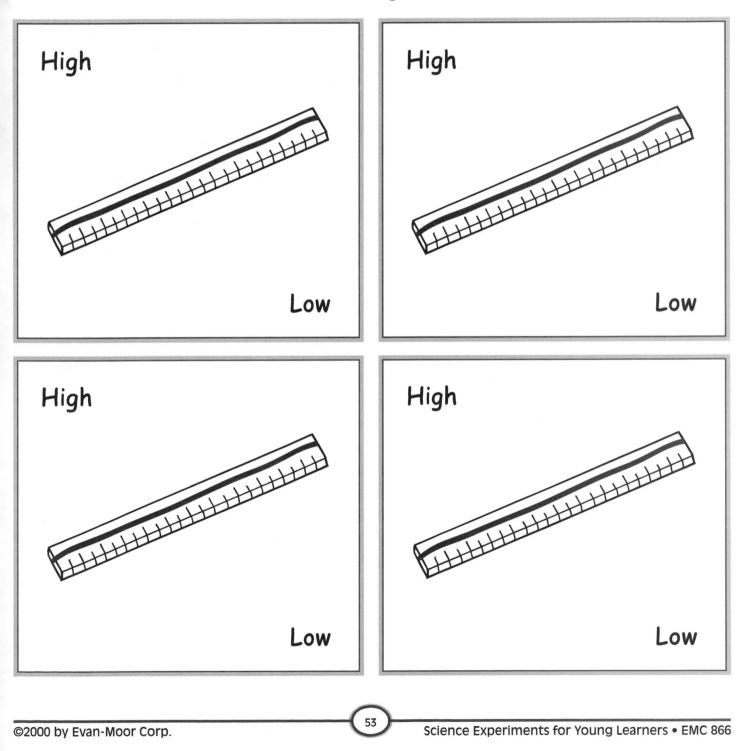

Science Experiments for Young Learners • EMC 866

Seeing Sound

Position and Motion of Objects

Sound is produced by vibrating objects.
Students observe that sound can cause nearby objects to vibrate.

Doing the Experiment

1. Cut a balloon and stretch it across the top of the open coffee can. Secure it with a rubber band.

2. Place a teaspoon of sugar in the center of the balloon.

3. Hold a metal pan close to the can and bang on the pan with a spoon.

4. Observe what happens. Record observations on the record sheet.

Sharing the Results

Discuss what happened. Ask, "What made the sugar move?"

The sound waves created by banging on the pan caused the balloon to vibrate and moved the sugar.

Making Connections

Explain that the balloon stretched across the coffee can is like an eardrum. Sound waves cause the membrane to vibrate. Those vibrations move along three little bones (the middle ear) to reach nerves. The nerves take information about the sound to the brain.

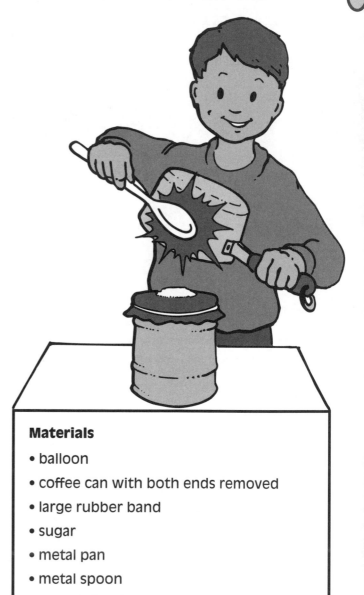

Materials

• balloon

• coffee can with both ends removed

• large rubber band

• sugar

• metal pan

• metal spoon

• record sheet on page 55, reproduced for individual students

Science Experiments for Young Learners • EMC 866

Name _____

Seeing Sound

Cut and paste to tell what happened.

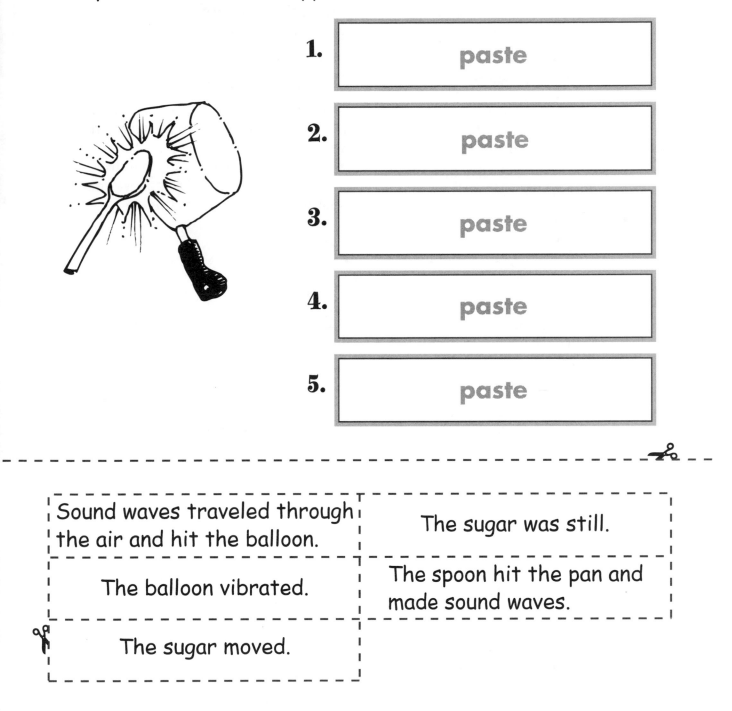

1. paste

2. paste

3. paste

4. paste

5. paste

Sound waves traveled through the air and hit the balloon.

The sugar was still.

The balloon vibrated.

The spoon hit the pan and made sound waves.

The sugar moved.

Science Experiments for Young Learners • EMC 866

A Howler-Growler

Position and Motion of Objects

Sound is produced by vibrating objects.
Students experiment to make sound louder.

Doing the Experiment

1. Make one howler-growler to demonstrate or have each student make their own howler-growler.

   - Use the nail to poke a small hole in the bottom of the cup.

   - Push one end of the string through the hole and into the cup.

   - Tie the button onto the end of the string that is inside the cup.

   - Pull the string back through the hole until the button is flat against the inside bottom of the cup.

2. Hold the cup right-side up with the fingers of one hand.

3. Grasp the string coming out the bottom of the cup between the thumb and the forefinger.

4. Pull downward on the string, letting it jerk through your thumb and finger.

Sharing the Results

Have students explain what they heard and why they think the sound occurred.

As the string slides through the fingers, it begins to vibrate. The string causes the button to vibrate the bottom of the cup. Sound waves are created. The shape of the cup concentrates and amplifies the sound waves.

Making Connections

Compare the howler-growler to a violin. The sound that is created by sliding the fingers down the thread is like the sound that comes from a violin string as the bow is pulled across it. The hollow violin body amplifies the sound the same way the hollow cup does.

Materials

- for each howler-growler:
  button
  paper cup
  nail, push pin, or sharpened pencil
  12" (31 cm) piece of thread or kite string

- picture directions on page 57, reproduced as a transparency or for individual students

Science Experiments for Young Learners • EMC 866

Picture Directions for Making a Howler-Growler

Physical Science

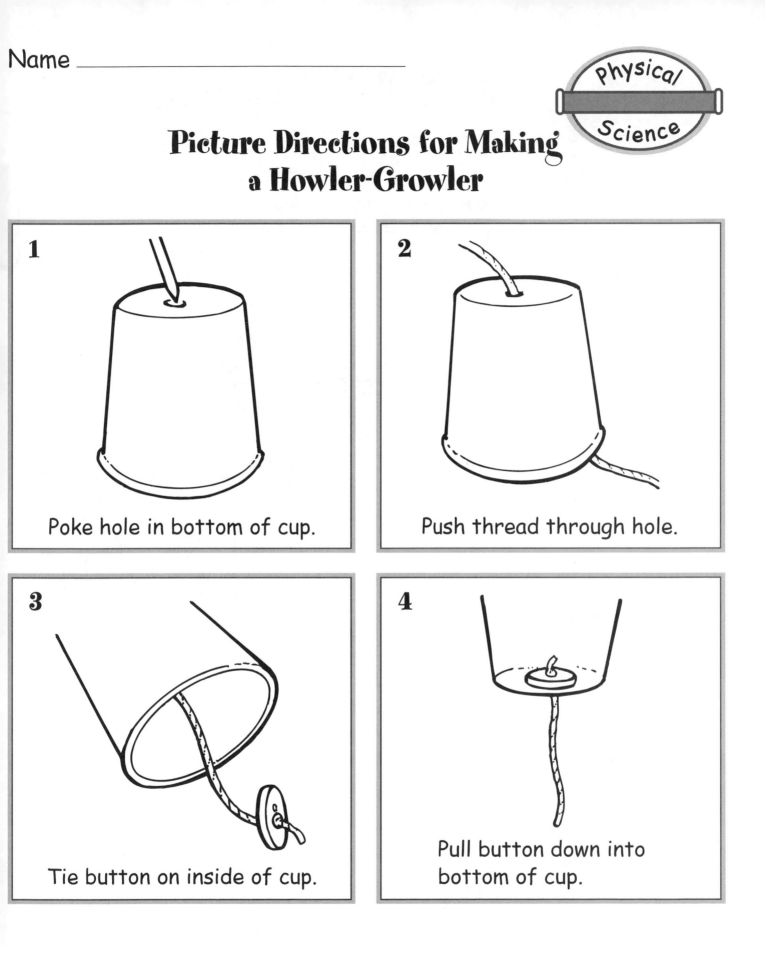

1 Poke hole in bottom of cup.

2 Push thread through hole.

3 Tie button on inside of cup.

4 Pull button down into bottom of cup.

Super Listener Earphones

Position and Motion of Objects

Sound is produced by vibrating objects.
Students confirm that an object must begin vibrating before sound is produced.

Doing the Experiment

1. Each pair of students will make a set of earphones.

   • Use the nail to make a hole in the bottom of each cup.

   • Cut the string in half. Put one end of each string through the hole in the bottom of each cup.

   • Tie the string ends inside the cups to paper clips.

2. Follow the directions on the task cards to listen to different vibrations.

Sharing the Results

Talk about the sounds students heard through the earphones. Ask, "Did the Slinky® make any noise before it was tapped? What about the hanger? the fork? the spoon? What was the same about all the sounds?"

Record student responses on a chart or chalkboard. Guide students to generalize the idea that when the objects were plucked or tapped there were sounds. The object had to start vibrating before the sound was audible.

Making Connections

Have students find other objects in the classroom that make noise when they vibrate.

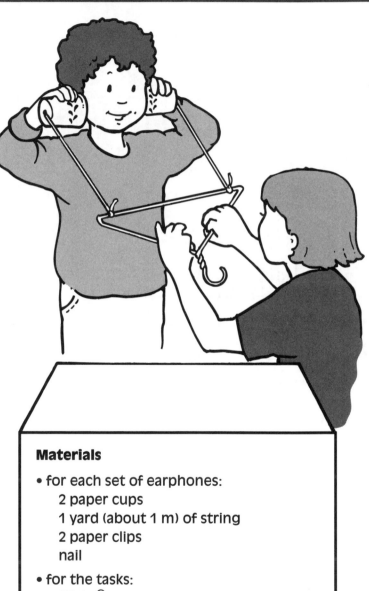

Materials

• for each set of earphones:
   2 paper cups
   1 yard (about 1 m) of string
   2 paper clips
   nail

• for the tasks:
   Slinky®
   metal coat hanger
   fork
   spoon

• task cards on page 59

Science Experiments for Young Learners • EMC 866

Listening to Vibrations

Task 1

Tie the earphones near the middle of the Slinky®.

Put the cups to your ears and listen.

Pluck one end of the Slinky®.

Listen again.

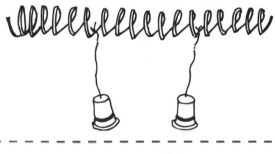

Task 2

Tie an earphone to each end of a hanger.

Put both cups to your ears and listen.

Tap the middle of the hanger.

Listen again.

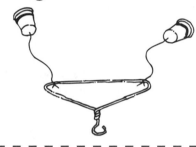

Task 3

Tie both of the earphone strings to a fork handle.

Put the cups to your ears and listen.

Tap the tines of the fork.

Listen again.

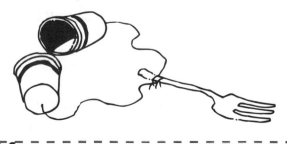

Task 4

Tie both of the earphone strings to the spoon handle.

Put both cups to your ears and listen.

Tap the bowl of the spoon.

Listen again.

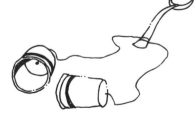

Science Experiments for Young Learners • EMC 866

Making Water Music

Position and Motion of Objects

Sound is produced by vibrating objects.

Students observe that the pitch of a sound can be changed by increasing or decreasing the size of a column of air.

Doing the Experiment

1. Demonstrate how to make and use a bottle xylophone.

   - Remove the caps and labels from the bottles.

   - Pour different amounts of water into the bottles.

   - Tap the sides of the bottles with the pencil.

2. Have students make their own xylophones or take turns using the class set.

3. Challenge students to line up the bottles so the tones range from the lowest on the left to the highest on the right. Students then complete their record sheets.

Sharing the Results

Ask, "Why did the bottles make different tones when they were tapped? What is the relationship between the amount of water and the tone?"

The pitch of a sound can be changed by increasing or decreasing the size of the column of air.

Making Connections

Consider these questions: "Does the thickness of the glass affect the sound? Do you get the same tones using the same amount of other liquids like milk or cooking oil?"

Materials

- water
- plastic measuring cup
- pencil
- 8 identical glass soft drink or juice bottles
- record sheet on page 61, reproduced for individual students

Science Experiments for Young Learners • EMC 866

Name _____

Making Water Music

Draw the water in the bottles.

Highest

Lowest

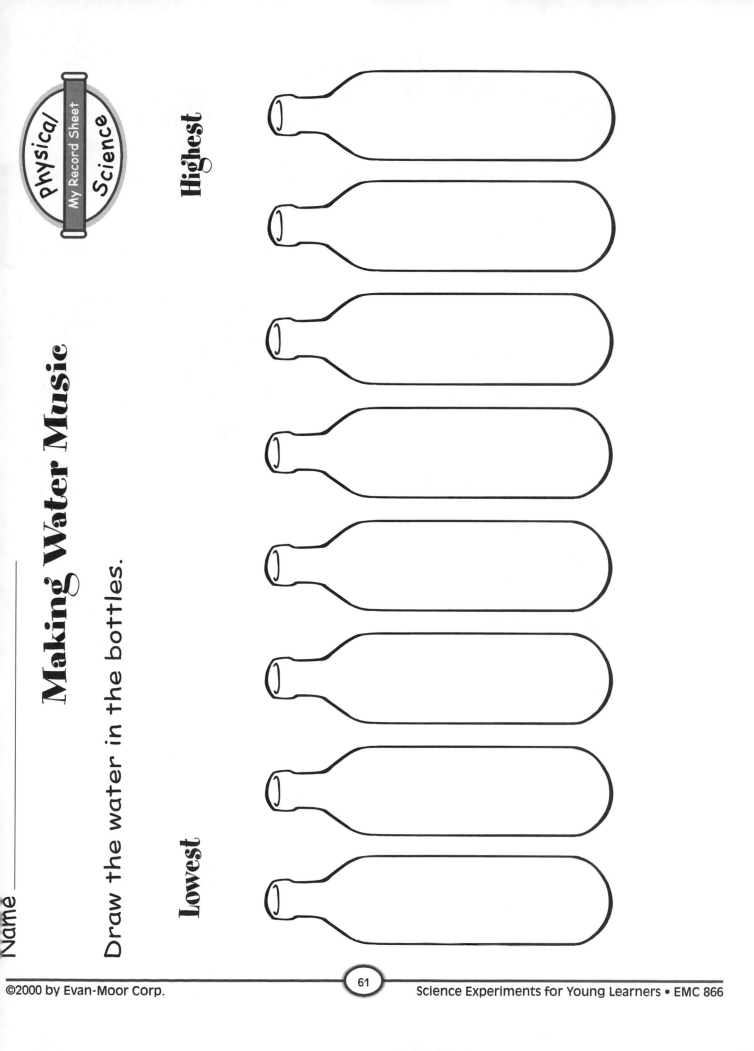

Science Experiments for Young Learners • EMC 866

Where Will the Light Go?

Light, Heat, Electricity, & Magnetism

Light travels in a straight line.

Students predict where light will go and observe to confirm their predictions.

Doing the Experiment

1. Four students stand at the front of the classroom.

2. Stand across the classroom with a flashlight.

3. Show how you will hold the flashlight. (Point it at student's chest.)

4. Ask students to predict where the light will go.

5. Turn off the room light and turn on the flashlight.

6. Repeat the experiment several times.

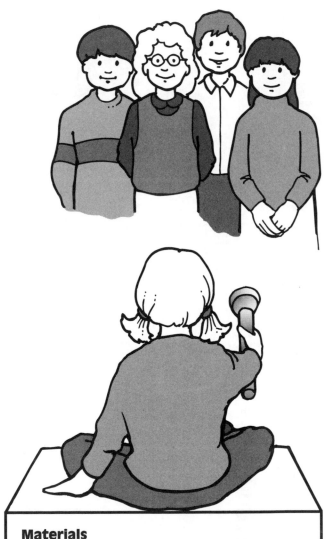

Sharing the Results

Discuss whether the students' predictions were correct. Ask "How did you know where the light would go?"

Making Connections

Have students think of things that are caught in a spotlight's beam (*ringmaster in the circus, deer in headlights, actor on a stage*).

Students complete the activity sheet to show they understand that light travels in a straight line.

Materials

- flashlight
- activity sheet on page 63, reproduced for individual students

　　Science Experiments for Young Learners • EMC 866

Name _____

Where Will the Light Go?

Draw the rays of light coming from the light source to show where they will go.

Block the Light

Light, Heat, Electricity, & Magnetism

Light can be blocked.

Students experiment to discover that the path of light can be blocked.

Doing the Experiment

Note: You will need to do steps 1 through 3 in advance.

1. Make the same size hole in the center of each piece of cardboard.

2. Using thumbtacks, attach the cardboard pieces to the wooden blocks.

3. Place the standing cardboard pieces, one in front of the other, about 6" (15 cm) apart. Make sure that the holes are in a straight line.

4. Hold the flashlight in front of the first cardboard piece. Adjust the light so it shines directly through the holes.

5. Darken the room and turn on the flashlight. Hold a piece of black construction paper in back of the last piece of cardboard. Clap chalk erasers together over the row of cardboard pieces to make the beam of light more visible.

6. Move one piece of cardboard so that the hole is not lined up with the others. Have students predict what will happen.

7. Turn on the flashlight to test their predictions.

Sharing the Results

Talk with students about what they observed. Then have students complete their record sheets.

Making Connections

Ask students to explain how this experiment is like pulling a blind over a window to block the light. Can your students think of other examples of blocked light?

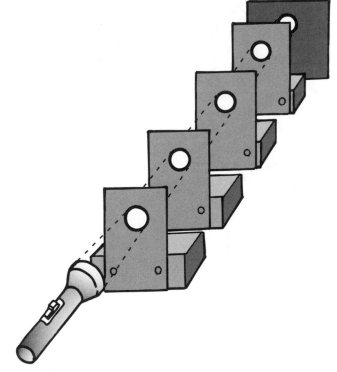

Materials

- flashlight
- 4 blocks of wood
- thumbtacks
- chalk erasers
- 4 equal-sized pieces of cardboard
- black construction paper or dark surface on wall
- record sheet on page 65, reproduced for individual students

Science Experiments for Young Learners • EMC 866

Name _____

Block the Light

Use a crayon. Draw the light to show the path that it traveled each time.

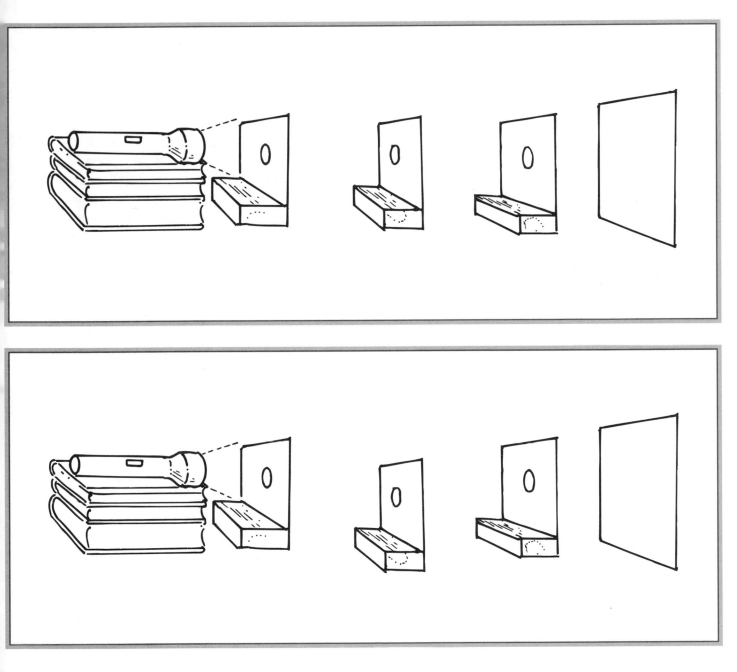

Science Experiments for Young Learners • EMC 866

Spots of Light

Light, Heat, Electricity, & Magnetism

Light can be reflected.

Students experiment with mirrors to reflect light in different directions.

Doing the Experiment

1. Give each student a mirror. Students should spread out in the classroom.

2. Challenge them to use their mirrors to make spots of light on the ceiling or the wall.

3. Ask questions such as these to encourage problem solving as they work:

   "What shape is your light spot?"

   "Can you change its shape?"

   "Can you change the size of your light spot? How?"

   "Can you make a light spot in a dark part of the room?"

   "Can you make a light spot in a light part of the room?"

   "Can you make a spot on the chalkboard, the door, or the floor?"

   "How do you hold your mirror to make a light spot?"

Sharing the Results

Have students demonstrate the ways they change the direction of a beam of light. Encourage multiple solutions to a single question. Then have students complete their record sheets.

Making Connections

Explain that when light bounces off an object, we say it is *reflected*. Show a bicycle reflector. Ask students to explain why people have reflectors on their bikes. Have students think of other ways reflecting light can help people *(reflecting strips on runners, pet collars that reflect, reflecting strips along highway medians and on signs)*.

Materials

- nonbreakable aluminum mirrors

- a bright light source (an overhead projector, a lamp, a high-power flashlight, or sunlight)

- record sheet on page 67, reproduced for individual students

Science Experiments for Young Learners • EMC 866

Name _____

Spots of Light

Draw a picture. Show how the light traveled to make your spot of light. Show:

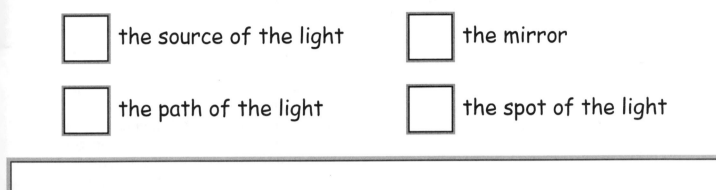

the source of the light   the mirror

the path of the light   the spot of the light

Science Experiments for Young Learners • EMC 866

Reflecting Light

Light, Heat, Electricity, & Magnetism

Light can be reflected.

Students experiment to discover that when the angle of a mirror is changed, the reflected light changes.

Doing the Experiment

1. Make a beam blocker.

   • Cut a "bite" out of the piece of cardboard about 1" (2.5 cm) in diameter.

   • Tape a comb across the bite.

2. Darken the room.

3. Place the beam blocker in front of a flashlight so that the narrow beams of light travel through the teeth of the comb.

4. Hold a mirror in the beams of light so that the mirror reflects the light.

5. Move the mirror to a different angle. Note how the reflected light changes.

Sharing the Results

Ask your students, "What happens to the beams of light? How does changing the position of the mirror change what happens to the light?" Draw a diagram on the record sheet to show how the direction of the light rays are changed by the mirror.

Light is reflected by a mirror at exactly the same angle as it hits a mirror.

Making Connections

Ask students to think of places where they have seen reflections *(lake, mirror, shiny toaster)*. To help students understand how light bounces off a surface and is reflected, bounce a ball against a wall. Explain to students that light is like the ball. Light bounces off surfaces and travels back the same way it came unless something gets in its way. The bouncing back of a ray of light from a surface is called *reflection*. Have students compare the ball and the light beam.

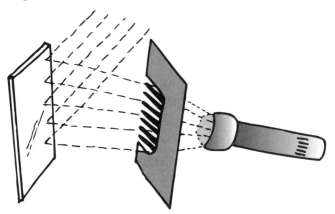

Materials
• for each beam blocker:
    piece of cardboard
    comb
    tape
• flashlight
• mirror
• record sheet on page 69, reproduced for individual students

Science Experiments for Young Learners • EMC 866

Name _____

Reflecting Light

Draw the beam of light. Show how it changes directions.

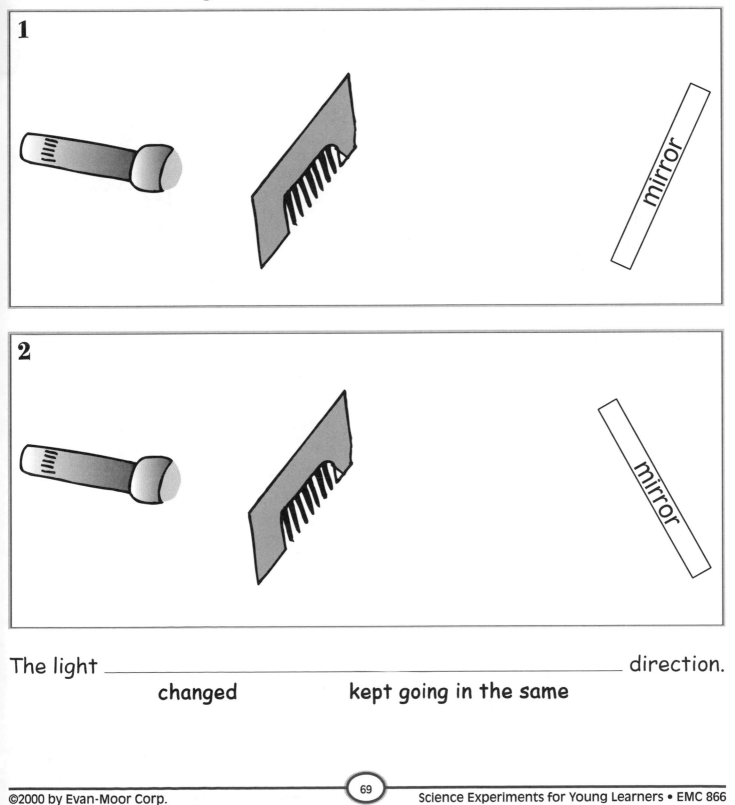

The light _____ direction.

       changed   **kept going in the same**

Make a Periscope

Light, Heat, Electricity, & Magnetism

Light can be reflected by a mirror.

Students discover that they can look around corners using reflected light.

Doing the Experiment

1. Make the periscope.

   • Cut a viewing hole near the bottom of one end of the cardboard tube or box.

   • Cut a second viewing hole on the opposite side of the other end.

   • Position the hand mirrors inside the tube or box at each end.

   • Cut slits so that the mirrors stay in place.

2. Look through the periscope to see around corners or over objects. You may want to set up a discovery station with several periscopes and rotate students through the station.

Sharing the Results

Draw a cross section of the periscope on the chalkboard. Ask students to figure out how the light rays move through the periscope. Draw the lines of light with chalk. Have students complete their individual periscope drawings on the record sheet.

Making Connections

Ask students to think of ways a periscope could be used (*submarine commanders can find out what is happening above the surface by raising a periscope out of the water*).

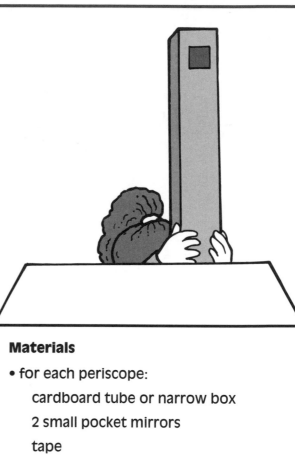

Materials

• for each periscope:

   cardboard tube or narrow box

   2 small pocket mirrors

   tape

• record sheet on page 71, reproduced for individual students

Science Experiments for Young Learners • EMC 866

Using a Periscope

Draw yourself looking through the periscope. Draw a picture to show what you see.

Draw lines to show how the light moved through the periscope.

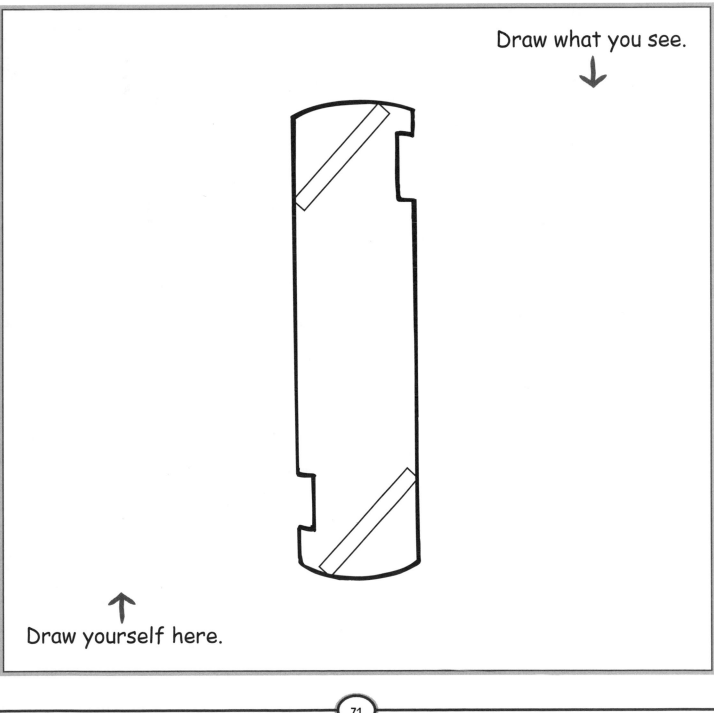

Draw what you see.

Draw yourself here.

Making Shadows

Light travels in a straight line until it strikes an object.

Students experiment to learn that shadows are formed when light is blocked.

Doing the Experiment

1. Students sit in front of the light source facing the wall.

2. Hold objects in front of the light source one at a time.

3. Students guess what the object is without looking.

Sharing the Results

Ask the students to explain how they were able to identify each object. Help students generalize the idea that an object blocks light rays. We see a shadow where the light is blocked. The shadow is the same shape as the object.

Making Connections

Look at the shadows and objects on the activity sheet. Have students match objects with their shadows.

Materials

- light-colored wall or bulletin board
- projector or other light source
- familiar objects (fork, spatula, scissors, pencil, cup)
- activity sheet on page 73, reproduced for individual students

Science Experiments for Young Learners • EMC 866

Name _____

Making Shadows

Draw lines to match the objects with the shadows they make.

Science Experiments for Young Learners • EMC 866

Feeling Heat

Light, Heat, Electricity, & Magnetism

Heat can be produced in many ways.

Students complete four tasks to discover that there are many sources of heat.

Before the experiment, set up these four task stations:

Task Station 1—direction card, a bowl of warm water, towel

Task Station 2—direction card, egg timer

Task Station 3—direction card, heating pad

Task Station 4—direction card, block of wood, sandpaper

Doing the Experiment

Students complete four tasks. After each task, students should draw a picture and/or write a sentence to tell what they did and what they felt.

1. Students dip their hands into warm water.

2. Students rub their hands together.

3. Students lay their hands on a heating pad.

4. Students sand a block of wood with a piece of sandpaper.

Sharing the Results

Have students share their experiences. Ask "What is the same about what you felt after each task?" Help students conclude that they felt heat while doing each task.

Making Connections

Have students list as many sources of heat as they can. Record the ideas on a chart or in a class logbook.

Materials

- egg timer
- towel
- sandpaper
- bowl or tub of warm water
- direction cards on page 75, reproduced for task stations
- heating pad
- block of wood

Science Experiments for Young Learners • EMC 866

Direction Cards

Task 1

Dip your hands in the water.

Task 2

Rub your hands together until the timer is done.

Task 3

Feel the heating pad.

Task 4

Sand the block of wood.

Science Experiments for Young Learners • EMC 866

Light, Heat, Electricity, & Magnetism

Magnets attract and repel each other and other materials.

Students predict which objects a magnet will pick up and then experiment to confirm their predictions.

Doing the Experiment

1. Show the objects to be used in the experiment.

2. Ask students to predict which objects will be attracted to the magnet. Record the predictions.

3. Students use their magnets to try to pick up each object.

4. Students record the results on their record sheets. Circle each object the magnet picked up. Cross out each object the magnet did not pick up.

Sharing the Results

Students tell which objects they were able to pick up with their magnets. Put all the objects that were picked up together on a table. Ask, "How are all these the same?"

Making Connections

Students take the magnets around the classroom and playground to find other objects that are attracted to a magnet. (Note: Be sure to tell students that they should not hold up a magnet to a TV or computer screen.)

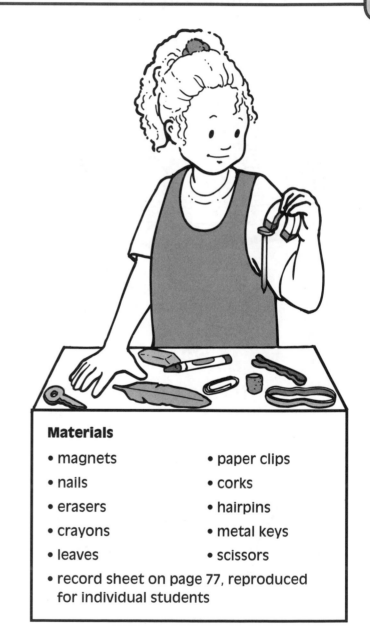

Materials

- magnets
- nails
- erasers
- crayons
- leaves
- paper clips
- corks
- hairpins
- metal keys
- scissors
- record sheet on page 77, reproduced for individual students

Science Experiments for Young Learners • EMC 866

Name _____

Magnet Magic

©2000 by Evan-Moor Corp.   Science Experiments for Young Learners • EMC 866

Metals Aren't All the Same

Light, Heat, Electricity, & Magnetism

Magnets attract and repel each other and other materials.
Students experiment to find out if magnets attract all metal objects.

Doing the Experiment

1. Ask students to name and describe each of the objects. "What are all of these made from? Will a magnet pick up all of these objects? Will a magnet pick up anything that is metal?" Record the predictions.

2. Students try to pick up each object with their magnets.

3. Record the results on the record sheet. Circle the objects that can be picked up. Cross out objects that cannot be picked up.

Sharing the Results

Ask "Did your magnet pick up all the metal objects? Which kind of metal objects are attracted to the magnet?"

(You may want to help students generalize that only metals such as iron and steel are attracted to a magnet.)

Making Connections

Have students list all the metal objects in their desk or work area. Then test each object to see if it is attracted to a magnet.

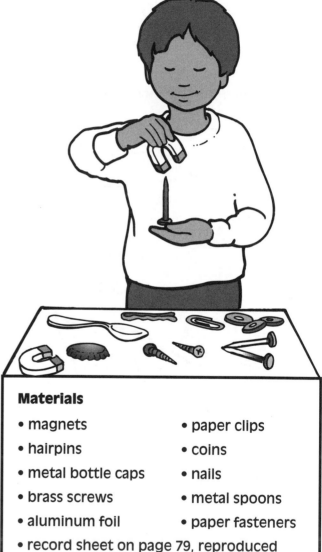

Materials

- magnets
- hairpins
- metal bottle caps
- brass screws
- aluminum foil
- paper clips
- coins
- nails
- metal spoons
- paper fasteners
- record sheet on page 79, reproduced for individual students

Science Experiments for Young Learners • EMC 866

Name _____

Metals Aren't
All the Same

Testing a Magnet's Strength

Light, Heat, Electricity, & Magnetism

Magnets attract and repel each other and other materials.
Students find out which magnets are the strongest.

Doing the Experiment

1. Students make predictions. "How many paper clips do you think your magnet will pick up?" Record the predictions.

2. Each student uses a different magnet. Each picks up as many paper clips as possible.

3. Students record the results on their record sheets. Cut out the correct number of paper clips and paste to the picture of the magnet.

Sharing the Results

Each student shows how many paper clips were picked up. "Which magnet was the strongest?" Order the record sheets to show the magnet that picked up the most paper clips. Compare the results with the predictions.

Making Connections

Ask, "What kinds of jobs would need a strong magnet?" If possible, invite a worker who uses large industrial magnets to your classroom to describe the jobs that super magnets do.

Materials

- paper clips
- magnets—You will need one for each student. Magnets should be different sizes and shapes.
- record sheet on page 81, reproduced for individual students

Name _____

Strong Magnets

My magnet picked up _____ paper clips.

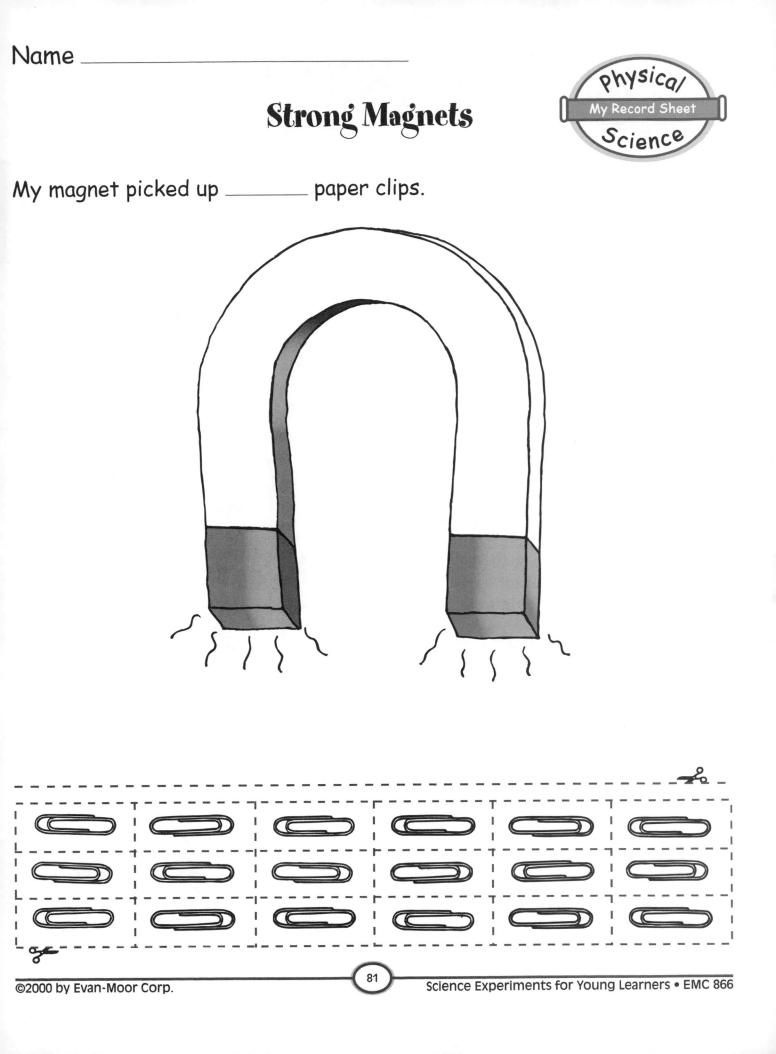

The Force Moves Through

Light, Heat, Electricity, & Magnetism

Magnets attract and repel each other and other materials.

Students experiment to find out if magnets can attract objects through various kinds of materials.

Doing the Experiment

1. Put a paper clip in a glass. Move the magnet along the outside of the glass. Ask, "Does the paper clip move?" Record the results on the record sheet by circling "yes" if the magnet attracts the paper clip or "no" if it does not.

2. Put the paper clip under a sheet of paper. Place the magnet on the paper. Try to lift up the paper and the paper clip. Record the results on the record sheet.

3. Put the paper clip under a piece of cloth. Place the magnet on top of the cloth. Try to lift up the cloth and the paper clip. Record the results on the record sheet.

4. Put the paper clip on top of a tongue depressor. Lift up the tongue depressor and put the magnet under it. Move the magnet to see if the paper clip will move. Record the results on the record sheet.

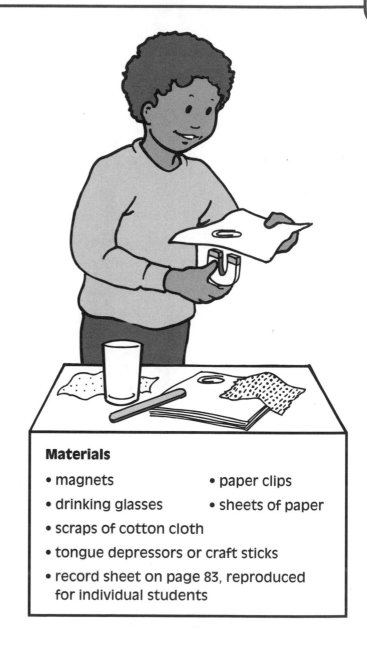

Sharing the Results

Ask, "Did the magnet move the paper clip through all the different materials?" Have students share their record sheets.

Making Connections

Try the same experiment using thicker wood, cardboard, and heavier cloth.

Materials

- magnets
- drinking glasses
- scraps of cotton cloth
- tongue depressors or craft sticks
- record sheet on page 83, reproduced for individual students
- paper clips
- sheets of paper

Science Experiments for Young Learners • EMC 866

Name _____

The Force Moves Through

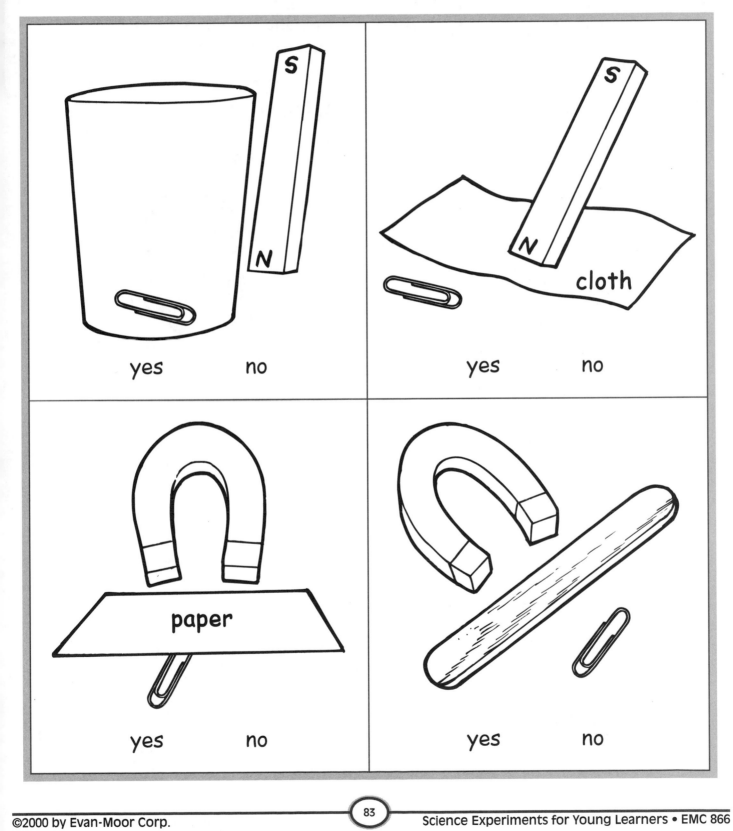

yes   no

yes   no

cloth

paper

yes   no

yes   no

Science Experiments for Young Learners • EMC 866

Attract and Repel

Light, Heat, Electricity, & Magnetism

Magnets attract and repel each other and other materials.

Students experiment to discover that like poles of magnets repel each other and unlike poles attract each other.

Doing the Experiment

1. Tie a piece of thread to the center of two bar magnets.

2. Hold the magnets by the threads so that they can turn freely.

3. Move ends of the magnets near each other and note what happens:
   • north end to north end
   • north end to south end
   • south end to south end

   Students record the results in the top two boxes on their record sheets.

4. Move the full length of the magnets toward each other and note what happens:
   • same poles together
   • opposite poles together

   Students record the results in the bottom two boxes on their record sheets.

Sharing the Results

Students share results. Help them generalize what they have observed.

When the like poles were close together, the magnet on the string was repelled by the second magnet. When the unlike poles were close together, the magnet on the string was attracted to the second magnet.

Making Connections

If possible, show some self-closing cupboard latches that use magnets to help them close.

Materials

• heavy thread or string

• two bar magnets (Note: Make sure that the bars are correctly magnetized and each has an *N* and an *S* marked on opposite ends.

• record sheet on page 85, reproduced for individual students

Science Experiments for Young Learners • EMC 866

Name _____

Will It Attract or Repel?

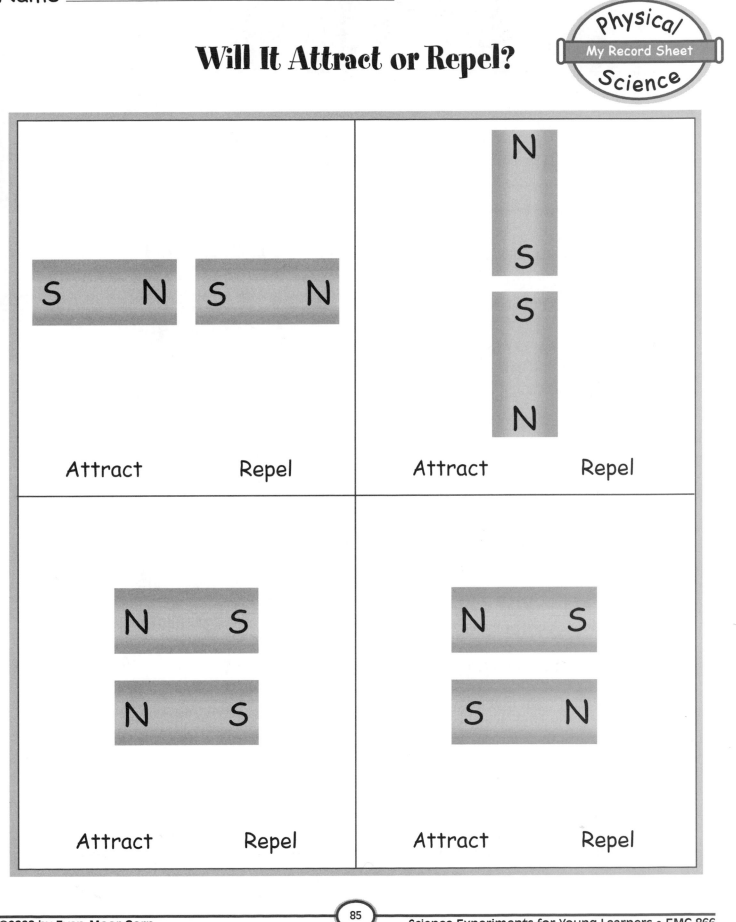

Attract   Repel

Attract   Repel

Attract   Repel

Attract   Repel

Science Experiments for Young Learners • EMC 866

Light It Up!

Light, Heat, Electricity, & Magnetism

Electrical circuits require a complete loop.

Students discover that an electric circuit must be complete in order for a light bulb to work.

Doing the Experiment

Note: The insulated wires should have the inner strands of metal showing at both ends.

1. Attach the wires to the two screws that are on the light socket.

2. Attach the other ends of the wires to the two terminals on the battery.

3. Observe what happens to the light bulb.

4. Detach one wire. Ask, "What happens to the light bulb?"

5. Reattach the wire. Ask, "What happens to the light bulb?"

6. Unscrew the light bulb. Ask, "What happens?"

7. Screw the light bulb back in.

Sharing the Results

Ask, "When was the light bulb lit? When was it not lit?" (The complete loop necessary to light the bulb is called an *electric circuit*.) Help students generalize that the circuit had to be complete in order for the light bulb to work. Have students complete their activity sheets.

Making Connections

Have students describe other electric circuits at work (*lights in the classroom, electric pencil sharpener, fan, computer*). Draw diagrams to show how the circuits are complete.

Materials

- insulated wire
- 6-volt battery
- small porcelain light socket with bulb
- activity sheet on page 87, reproduced for individual students

Caution: Batteries store electricity. Always use care when attaching wires to batteries.

Science Experiments for Young Learners • EMC 866

Name _____

Light It Up!

Draw the wires to make
a **complete** circuit.
What happens to the light?

light off   light on

Draw the wires to show
an **incomplete** circuit.
What happens to the light?

light off   light on

Think of another way to show an **incomplete** circuit. Draw it here.

Science Experiments for Young Learners • EMC 866

Name ______________________________

Physical Science

My Log

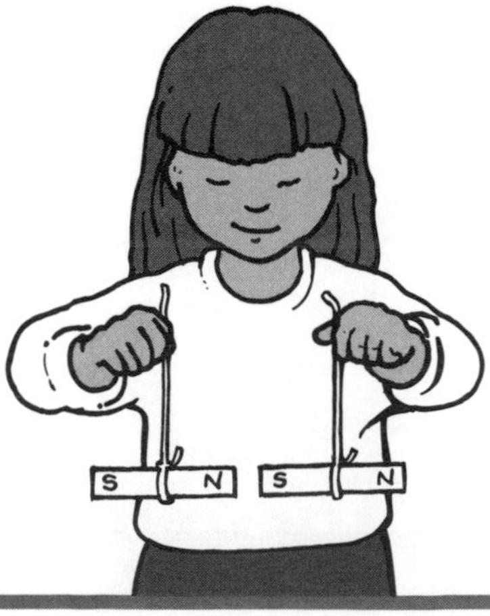

Life Science

- Living things have basic needs.

- Organisms can survive only in environments in which their needs can be met.

- Plants have different structures that serve different functions.

- Behavior is influenced by internal and external cues.

- Humans have senses that help them detect internal and external cues.

- Living things have a life cycle—being born, developing to adults, reproducing, and dying.

- Plants and animals closely resemble their parents.

- All animals depend on plants.

- Organisms cause changes in their environment.

Science Experiments for Young Learners • EMC 866

Growing Bags

Characteristics of Organisms

Living things have basic needs.
Students learn that seeds need water in order to germinate and grow.

Doing the Experiment

1. Fold the paper towel and place it in the bag. (It should touch the bottom of the bag.)

2. Draw a line across the bag about 2" (5 cm) from the bottom of the bag.

3. Staple through the bag and towels all along the line.

4. Drop the seeds into the bag.

5. Move the seeds so they are evenly spaced.

6. Tape or pin up the growing bag in the classroom where it will receive sunlight. (Do not add water to this bag.)

7. Follow the first five steps to make a second growing bag. This time add water to dampen the towels. (The towels should be kept damp by adding water as needed.)

8. Students observe the bags each day and record any changes they observe on their growing bag logs.

Sharing the Results

Ask, "What happened to the seeds in the dry growing bag? What happened to the seeds in the wet growing bag? Why was there a difference?"

Making Connections

Ask students to share their own planting experiences. Then ask, "Was water a factor in the success?"

Materials
- for each growing bag:
  4 bean seeds   white paper towel
  stapler   masking tape or pins
- 1 large (quart-size), self-closing plastic bag
- My Growing Bag Log on page 91, 2 copies for each student

Science Experiments for Young Learners • EMC 866

My Growing Bag Log

1. Cut along the dotted lines and fasten the strips together to make a number line.

2. Cut out the drawings of changes in the bean seed. Glue the first picture of the bean seed to Day 1.

3. Keep the other pictures in an envelope until they are needed.

4. As changes are observed, glue the correct picture on that day.

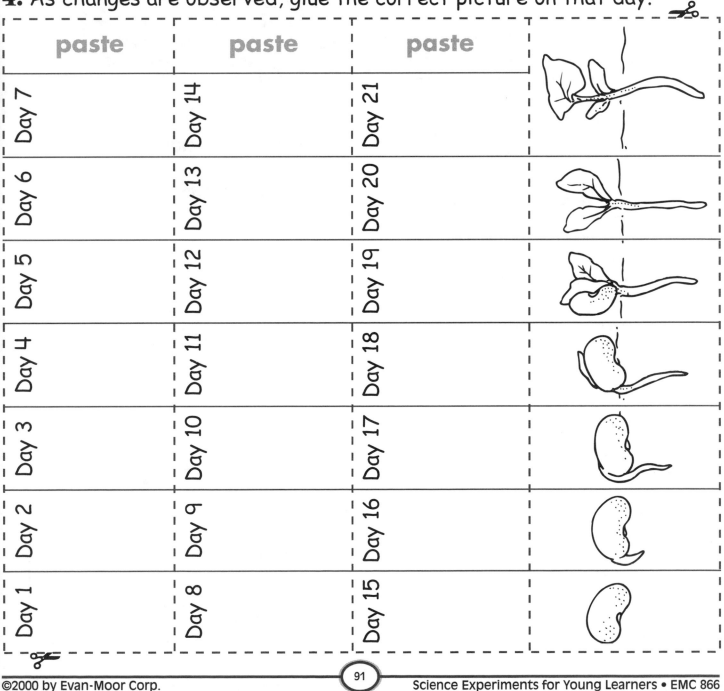

paste	paste	paste	
Day 7	Day 14	Day 21	
Day 6	Day 13	Day 20	
Day 5	Day 12	Day 19	
Day 4	Day 11	Day 18	
Day 3	Day 10	Day 17	
Day 2	Day 9	Day 16	
Day 1	Day 8	Day 15	

Science Experiments for Young Learners • EMC 866

Light or No Light?

Characteristics of Organisms

Living things have basic needs.

Students experiment to find out that plants need light to grow and survive.

Doing the Experiment

1. Soak the seeds in the saucer of water overnight. The seed coats will wrinkle and crack.

2. Fill the two flowerpots with soil. Leave about one inch of space at the top of each pot. Place five seeds, evenly spaced, on the surface. Cover the seeds with 1/2" (1.25 cm) of soil. Water thoroughly.

3. Put one pot in a dark place such as inside a closet or drawer. The plant needs to be in complete darkness. Even small amounts of light can change the results of the experiment.

4. Put the second pot in a sunny window.

5. Let the plants grow for 5 to 10 days. Water the seeds in each pot equally. (You will need to make sure that the room is completely dark when you open the closet or drawer to water the plant in the dark.)

6. When the plants in the sun are about six inches tall and have several leaves, bring the pot out of the darkness. Put the pots side by side.

7. Compare the plants. Record observations on the record sheet.

Sharing the Results

Ask, "Are the plants the same size? Is there a difference in color? How many leaves does each plant have?"

Plants growing in sunlight are green. The green color comes from chlorophyll. Together, sunlight and chlorophyll help plants produce their own food in a process called photosynthesis.

Making Connections

Put the plant grown in the dark in the sunny window. Ask, "What do you think will happen?" Watch the changes that occur.

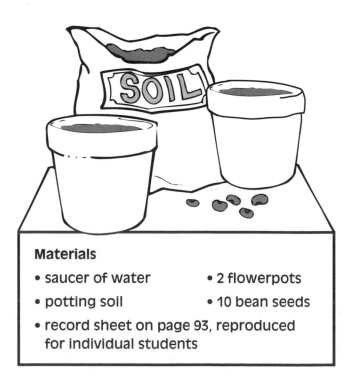

Materials
- saucer of water
- potting soil
- 2 flowerpots
- 10 bean seeds
- record sheet on page 93, reproduced for individual students

Science Experiments for Young Learners • EMC 866

Name _____

Light or No Light?

Draw the plants.

Growing in the Light	Growing with No Light

Write a sentence that explains the differences.

_____

_____

_____

_____

Light for Life

Characteristics of Organisms

Living things have basic needs.

Students learn that without light plants become unhealthy.

Doing the Experiment

1. Have students color the grass on their record sheets to match the patch of grass you will be using.

2. Lay the sheet of cardboard on a patch of grass. Leave it in place for a week.

3. Lift the cardboard and look at the grass beneath it. Students color their record sheets.

4. Take the cardboard away and wait another week. Students color their record sheets.

Sharing the Results

Have students share their record sheets. They should be able to discuss the concept that when sunlight was limited, the grass turned yellow and looked unhealthy. When the cardboard was removed, sunlight was no longer limited and the grass returned to normal.

Green plants need light from the sun to make their food. Without sunlight, green plants will die.

Materials

• sheet of heavy cardboard

• green, growing grass on playground

• record sheet on page 95, reproduced for individual students

Making Connections

Ask, "What might happen if a picnic table or lawn chair was left in one place for a long time?"

Science Experiments for Young Learners • EMC 866

Name _____

Light for Life

Draw to show what happened.

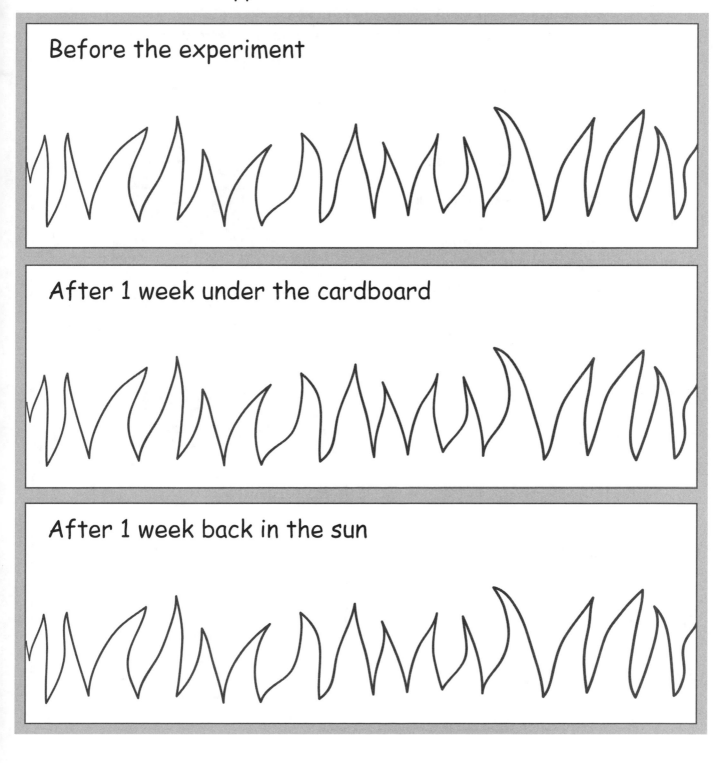

Before the experiment

After 1 week under the cardboard

After 1 week back in the sun

Science Experiments for Young Learners • EMC 866

Where Will It Grow Best?

Characteristics of Organisms

Organisms can survive only in environments in which their needs can be met.
Students experiment to find out if the growing medium affects plant growth.

Doing the Experiment

1. Line each basket with plastic wrap.

2. Pour one cup of a different planting material in each basket. Each student chooses a basket to observe and then records on the record sheet the planting material used.

3. Sprinkle 2 tablespoons of wheatberries on top of the planting materials.

4. Water until the water shows under the berries.

5. Cover each basket with plastic wrap. Put in a well-lighted place.

6. Remove the cover after two days.

7. Wait one week. Water if needed. Students make observations and record the growth that occurs.

Sharing the Results

Have students share record sheets and compare the growth of the grain in the different materials. Ask, "Is one material better for growing than another?"

Making Connections

Ask, "If you were going to plant a garden, what things would you want to think about before you planted your seeds?"

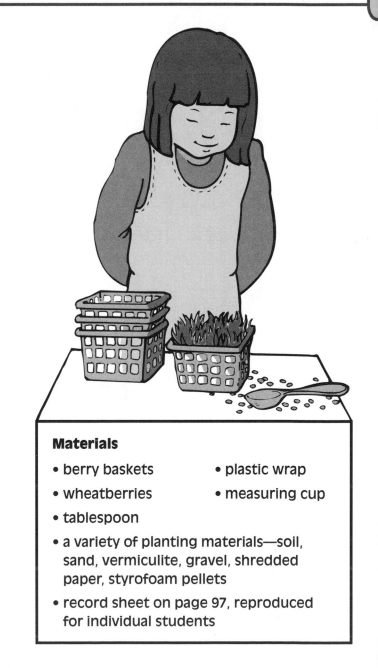

Materials

- berry baskets
- wheatberries
- tablespoon
- plastic wrap
- measuring cup
- a variety of planting materials—soil, sand, vermiculite, gravel, shredded paper, styrofoam pellets
- record sheet on page 97, reproduced for individual students

Science Experiments for Young Learners • EMC 866

Name _____

Where Will
It Grow Best?

Life
My Record Sheet
Science

Draw and write to show what happened.

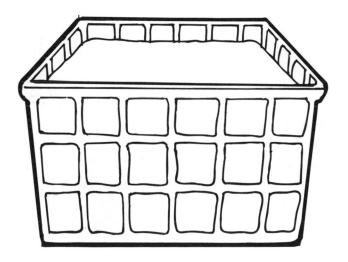

This is my basket.

It has _____ in it.

We planted seeds in it.

See how they grew.

I think this is a good place for growing seeds.   **yes**   **no**

97

Identifying the Parts of a Plant

Characteristics of Organisms

Plants have different structures that serve different functions.
Students learn the names for the various parts of a flowering plant.

Doing the Experiment

1. Divide your students into pairs or small groups. Give each group a potted plant.

2. Each group removes their plant from its container and removes the soil from around the roots. Lay the plant on the construction paper mat.

3. Name a plant part (root, stem, leaf, flower).

4. Have students locate each plant part on the real plants. Lay the labels beside the plant parts.

Sharing the Results

Take a photo of the labeled plant or have groups draw a picture to document their work. Discuss what the particular parts of the plant do to help the plant live and grow.

Labeling is a valuable authentic assessment.

Making Connections

Encourage students to label a different kind of plant or to collect several specimens of each plant part.

Materials

- several small flowering plants
- large spoons for removing plant from soil
- construction paper mat
- labels on page 99, reproduced for each group

Science Experiments for Young Learners • EMC 866

Plant Labels

roots	flower	stem	leaf
roots	flower	stem	leaf
roots	flower	stem	leaf
roots	flower	stem	leaf

   Science Experiments for Young Learners • EMC 866

With or Without Leaves?

Characteristics of Organisms

Plants have different structures that serve different functions in growth and survival.
Students learn that leaves are important to the growth of a plant.

Doing the Experiment

1. Remove all but one leaf from one of the plants.

2. Put the plants side by side in the same location. Care for them in the same way.

3. Observe the growth of the two plants.

4. Draw the plants on the record sheet at 3 days and 10 days.

Sharing the Results

Students share their drawings and their opinions on whether leaves are important to plant growth.

Making Connections

Try the experiment with different plants. Ask, "Are the leaves of all plants important?"

Materials

- 2 plants, the same kind, about the same size

- record sheet on page 101, reproduced for individual students

Science Experiments for Young Learners • EMC 866

Name _____

With or Without Leaves?

Plant 1

We took off all the leaves except one.

After 3 days

After 10 days

Plant 2

We left the leaves alone.

After 3 days

After 10 days

I think the leaves were   important   not important   to the plant.

Science Experiments for Young Learners • EMC 866

Colorful Carnations

Characteristics of Organisms

Plants have different structures that serve different functions in survival.
Students discover that plants have internal structures that move water through the plant.

Doing the Experiment

1. Fill the vases with water.

2. Put red food coloring in one vase, blue in the second, and yellow in the third.

3. Put a freshly cut white carnation in each vase.

4. Observe the flowers over the next few days.

5. Record any changes on the record sheet.

Sharing the Results

Ask, "How did the colored water get from the vase into the blossom?"

The colored water in the vase is carried through tubes in the stem to the flower (capillary action).

Making Connections

Seal the end of a carnation with plastic wrap and a rubber band. Put the flower in colored water. Predict what will happen. Ask, "How is the result of this experiment different from the first experiment? What does this experiment tell us about keeping cut flowers alive?"

Materials

- water
- 3 clear glass vases
- 3 white carnations
- red, blue, and yellow food coloring
- record sheet on page 103, reproduced for individual students

Name _____

Colorful Carnations

Color the drawings to show what happened.

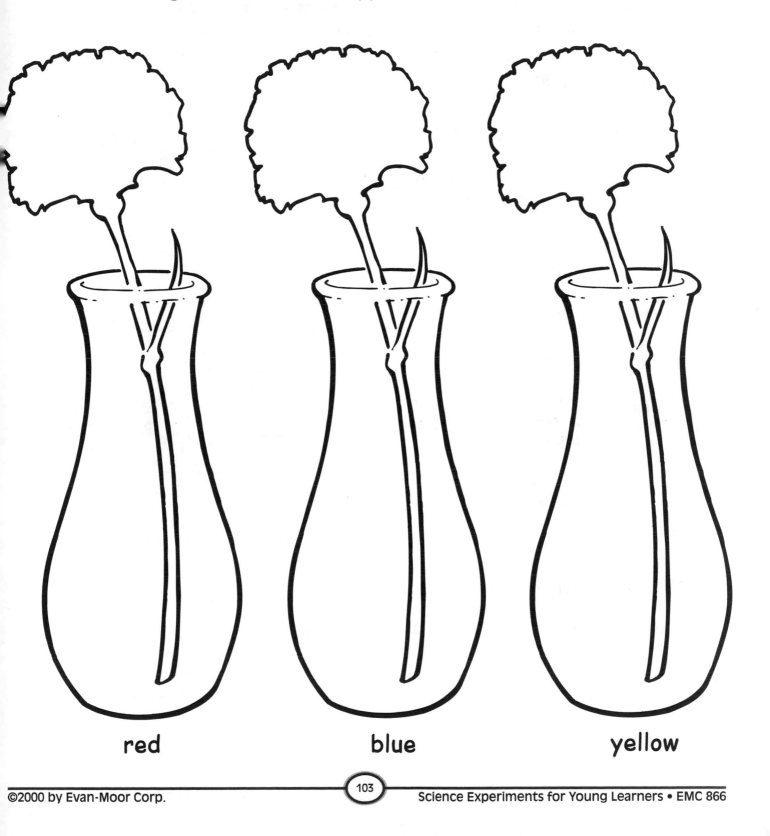

red   blue   yellow

Science Experiments for Young Learners • EMC 866

Super Seed

Characteristics of Organisms

Plants have different structures that serve different functions in growth and survival.
Students discover that a growing plant has considerable strength.

Doing the Experiment

1. Plant a bean seed in an egg carton cup.

2. Put a penny on top of the soil, right over the planted bean.

3. Place four toothpicks around the penny to keep it from falling to one side.

4. Keep the soil moist.

5. Watch what happens.

Measure the progress daily once the beans start sprouting and record the results on the record sheet.

Sharing the Results

Discuss how the penny was lifted by the growing seed. It's fun to plant more than one Super Seed and see which seed can lift the penny the highest.

The stem of a plant lifts and supports the leaves and fruits.

Making Connections

Ask, "When is it important for a plant to be able to lift something? Is it ever important for a plant to be able to lift soil or rocks? Can this ever cause problems?"

Materials

- bean seed
- penny
- 4 toothpicks
- soil
- egg carton
- record sheet on page 105, reproduced for individual students

Science Experiments for Young Learners • EMC 866

Name _____

Super Seed

Draw to show how your seed grows.

Day 1

Day 3

Day 6

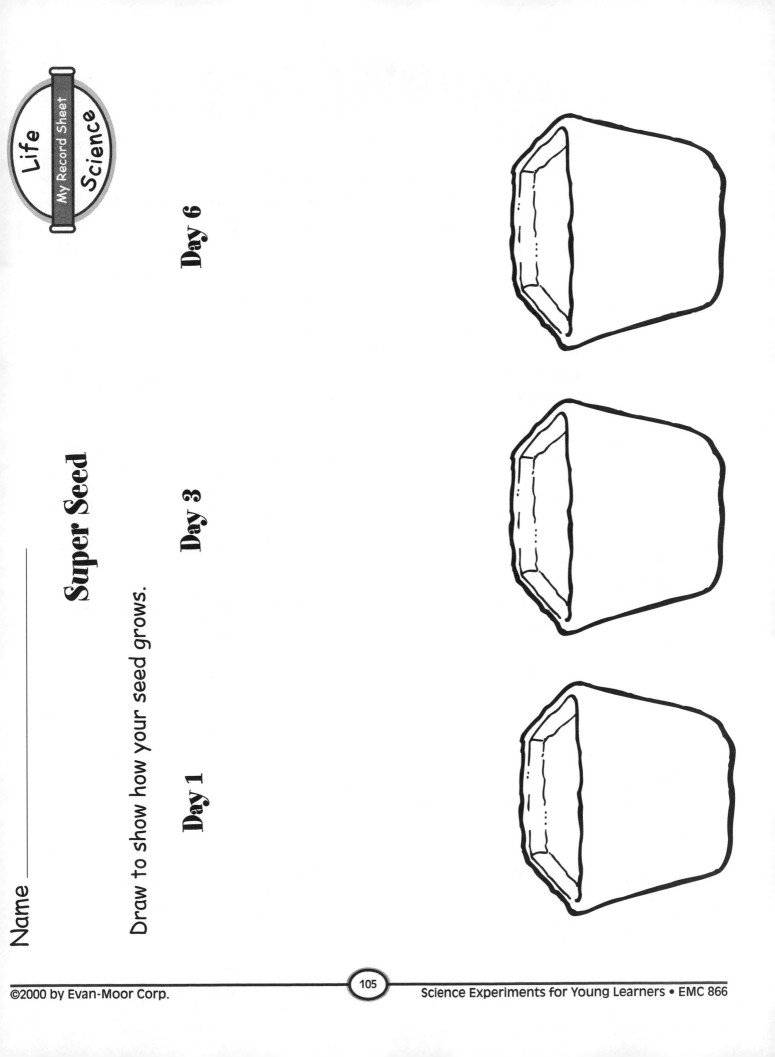

Science Experiments for Young Learners • EMC 866

Testing Seeds

Characteristics of Organisms

Plants have different structures that serve different functions in reproduction.
Students learn that not all seeds germinate.

Doing the Experiment

1. Fold the two sheets of paper towel on the perforation.

2. Moisten the towel slightly.

3. Lay a row of 5 seeds near the perforation line. Roll up the towel just past the seed row.

4. Lay 4 more rows of seeds in the same way. Roll up the towel as you lay out each row. (This makes 5 rows of 5 seeds.)

5. Finish rolling up the towel. Secure each end with a rubber band.

6. Draw a line on the jar about 1" (2.5 cm) from the bottom. This line is the water line. Add water to the jar to keep the water level even with this line.

7. Place the seed roll in the jar.

8. In about 5 days, unroll the towel one line of seeds at a time. On the record sheet, color the circles that correspond to the seeds that germinated.

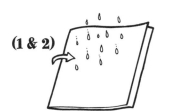

(1 & 2)

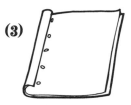

(3)

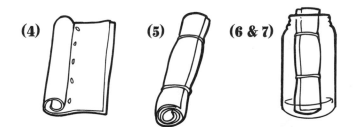

(4)   (5)   (6 & 7)

Sharing the Results

Have students complete their record sheets. Ask, "How many seeds germinated successfully?"

Making Connections

Ask, "How could gardeners use the results of this experiment when planting their gardens?"

Materials
- for each tester:
   water
   ruler
   jar or sturdy glass
   2 rubber bands
   marking pen
   25 seeds of a single variety
   2 sheets of paper towel not separated
- record sheet on page 107, reproduced for individual students

Science Experiments for Young Learners • EMC 866

Name _____

Testing Seeds

Color the circles to show the seeds that started to grow.

Science Experiments for Young Learners • EMC 866

Inside a Seed

Characteristics of Organisms

Plants have different structures that serve different functions in reproduction.
Students identify the embryo plant inside a bean seed.

Doing the Experiment

1. Put the seeds in a bowl of water and soak them for one night.

2. Take the seeds out of the water. Slip the seed coat off and open the seed carefully.

3. Use the magnifying glasses to look at the inside of the seeds. Ask, "What do you see?"

4. Students compare the drawing on the record sheet with what they see. They cut and paste to label the drawing and mark the structures they observed.

Sharing the Results

Help provide vocabulary for labeling as students tell about what they saw.

Making Connections

Try examining other seeds.

Materials

- bowl of water
- magnifying glasses
- lima beans (Note: You will want to have more beans than observers. The beans sometimes break as you open them.)
- record sheet on page 109, reproduced for individual students

Science Experiments for Young Learners • EMC 866

Name _____

Inside a Seed

Cut and paste to label the parts. Mark the ones you saw on the real bean seed.

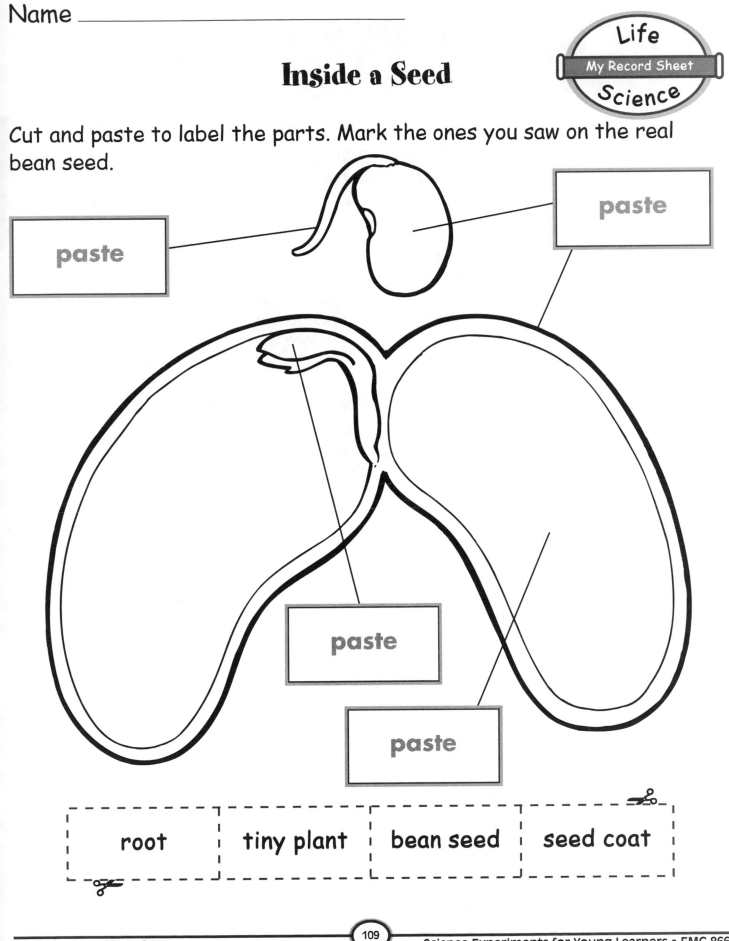

root | tiny plant | bean seed | seed coat

Science Experiments for Young Learners • EMC 866

Growing Toward the Sun

Characteristics of Organisms

Behavior is influenced by internal and external cues.

Students discover that plants grow toward light.

Doing the Experiment

1. Cut off the top of the box and turn it upside down. Seal any openings in the bottom of the box with masking tape. No light should leak through the seams of the box.

2. Cut a 2-inch square (5 cm) hole in one side of the box. Make the hole at about the same level as the base of the plant stem.

3. Place the plant on a desk or shelf near a sunny window. Put the box over the plant. Turn the box so that sunlight can enter the small hole. Place a similar plant beside the box. Do not cover the second plant.

4. Keep the boxed plant covered except when you need to water it. After about two weeks remove the box. Compare the boxed plant's growth to that of the plant sitting in the sun.

5. Students complete the record sheet.

Sharing the Results

Students should see that the stem of the boxed plant has started growing toward the hole in the box. Ask them to predict what they think will happen if the box is put back on the plant.

Plants produce a growth hormone called auxin in the stem tip. Auxin moves to the darker side of the plant, causing the cells to grow larger than the cells on the lighter side. This produces a curving of the plant tip toward light. This movement is called phototropism.

Making Connections

Try the same experiment with artificial light. Ask, "Does artificial light have the same effect on plants as the sun?"

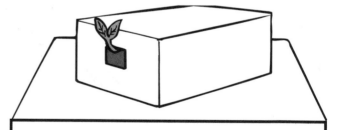

Materials

- masking tape
- sunny indoor location
- scissors or a box cutter
- cardboard box large enough to completely cover one plant
- small plants (bean plants grown in class work well or purchase some small squash plants)
- record sheet on page 111, reproduced for individual students

Science Experiments for Young Learners • EMC 866

Name _____

Growing Toward the Sun

Draw the plant to show what happened.

At first...

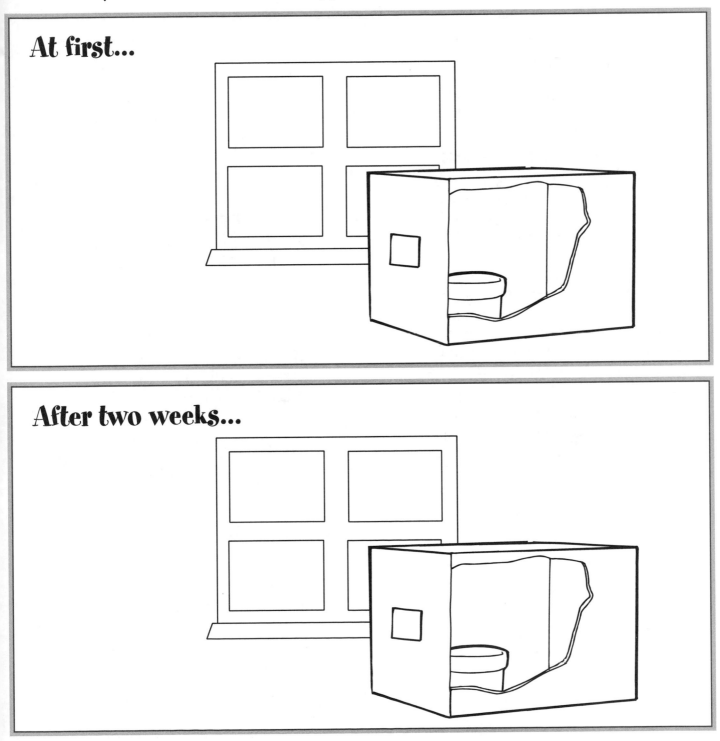

After two weeks...

My Five Senses—Seeing

Characteristics of Organisms

Humans have senses that help them detect internal and external cues.
Students experience that the sense of sight allows us to find out about our surroundings.

Doing the Experiment

1. Use the string to outline a circle about 5 feet (1.5 m) in diameter on a grassy area.

2. Scatter the candies inside the circle.

3. Have students work in pairs to locate the candies. They should stand outside the circle and map the location of the candies on their record sheet.

Sharing the Results

Ask, "Which sense did you use to find the candies?" After students respond that they used the sense of sight or seeing, ask, "Are some candies easier to find than others? Which were the hardest to see?"

Making Connections

Ask students to think of other times when the color of something makes it hard to see.

I found 2 red ones and 1 white one.

Materials

- grassy area
- string or rope
- candies in different-colored wrappings (Some of the wrappings should blend with the grass.)
- record sheet on page 113, reproduced for individual students

Science Experiments for Young Learners • EMC 866

Name _____

My Five Senses

I can use my sense of _____.

We put _____ candies on the grass. I stood outside the circle.

I found _____ candies.

Draw some of the candies that you found here.

I didn't see _____ candies.

Draw one of the candies you **didn't** find here.

I didn't find this candy because. . .

_____

_____

_____

 Science Experiments for Young Learners • EMC 866

My Five Senses—Feeling

Characteristics of Organisms

Humans have senses that help them detect internal and external cues.

Students experience that the sense of touch allows us to find out about properties of objects.

Doing the Experiment

1. Give each student a scavenger hunt list. Read over the list with students.

2. Go to the designated area. (This could be your classroom, a nature walk, a playground, or another indoor area.)

3. Students find the items on the list. Have them record their findings by checking off the item and writing or drawing what they found. (Some representative items could be collected and brought back to the classroom if you're doing an outdoors hunt. Or take your digital camera along and snap photos of the found items. Download them when you return to the classroom and create a multimedia record of your scavenger hunt.)

Sharing the Results

Discuss the hunt and the items that were found. Then ask, "What sense did you use to find the items? How did you know that the _____ was rough?"

Making Connections

Create a list of "touch" attributes—smooth, rough, hard, soft, scratchy, fuzzy—to use in writing activities.

Materials

- a designated area
- scavenger hunt list on page 115, reproduced for individual students

Science Experiments for Young Learners • EMC 866

Name _____

Scavenger Hunt List

□ something soft

□ something scratchy

□ something hard

□ something fuzzy

□ something smooth

□ something rough

Science Experiments for Young Learners • EMC 866

My Five Senses–Hearing

Characteristics of Organisms

Humans have senses that help them detect internal and external cues.
Students discover that objects can be identified by the sounds they make.

Doing the Experiment

1. Fill pairs of jars half full with each of the listed materials. Number the lids. Put on the lids and mix up the jars.

2. Students shake the jars to find two that sound alike.

3. Students record the numbers of the pairs and note the type of sounds they hear on their record sheets.

4. Take off the lids and check.

Sharing the Results

When all students have had a chance to match the pairs, ask, "What sense did you use to find the matching jars?"

Making Connections

Record familiar sounds on your tape recorder. Play the tape and have students identify what is making the sound.

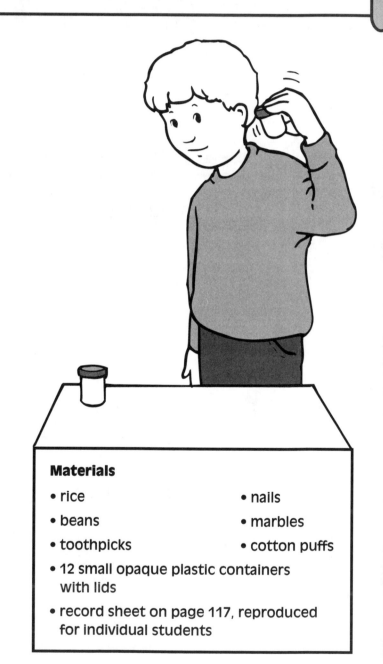

Materials

- rice
- beans
- toothpicks
- nails
- marbles
- cotton puffs
- 12 small opaque plastic containers with lids
- record sheet on page 117, reproduced for individual students

---

Science Experiments for Young Learners • EMC 866

Name _____

My Five Senses–Hearing

Number the containers to show which sound the same.

It sounded   loud   soft.

It sounded   loud   soft.

It sounded   loud   soft.

It sounded   loud   soft.

It sounded   loud   soft.

It sounded   loud   soft.

Science Experiments for Young Learners • EMC 866

My Five Senses–Smelling

Characteristics of Organisms

Humans have senses that help them detect internal and external cues.
Students discover that objects can be identified using the sense of smell.

Doing the Experiment

1. Apply each substance to two cotton balls.

2. Place one cotton ball in each jar. Cover the container with a circle of dark material. Use a rubber band to hold the cover in place. Write a number on each cover. Mix up the jars.

3. Students smell each container.

4. Students match like smells and record the numbers of the pairs on their record sheets.

Sharing the Results

After checking each of the paired containers, discuss with students what sense they used to make their pairings. Ask them if their senses of hearing and sight were helpful in making the matches.

Making Connections

Have students list examples of pleasant smells and unpleasant smells. Talk about how smell is beneficial.

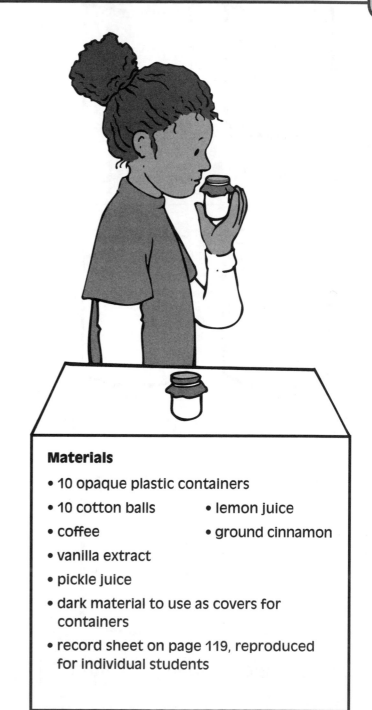

Materials

- 10 opaque plastic containers
- 10 cotton balls
- coffee
- lemon juice
- ground cinnamon
- vanilla extract
- pickle juice
- dark material to use as covers for containers
- record sheet on page 119, reproduced for individual students

Science Experiments for Young Learners • EMC 866

Name _____

My Five Senses–Smelling

Write the numbers of the matching jars.
Circle the word that tells about the smell.

It smelled   **good**   bad.

It smelled   **good**   bad.

It smelled   **good**   bad.

It smelled   **good**   bad.

It smelled   **good**   bad.

Science Experiments for Young Learners • EMC 866

My Five Senses–Tasting

Characteristics of Organisms

Humans have senses that help them detect internal and external cues.

Students use the sense of taste to sort objects into salty, sweet, and sour.

Doing the Experiment

1. Distribute sorting mats. Be sure students understand the three categories on the mat.

2. Students cut out the symbols representing each item.

3. Students taste each item and place the symbol in the appropriate area of the mat to describe its taste.

Sharing the Results

Students share their completed sorting mats. Discuss the three categories of tastes. Have students tell which category they like best.

Making Connections

Have students collect illustrations from magazines representing foods that are salty, sweet, and sour.

Materials

- bowls of taste samples:
    tortilla chips
    salted sunflower seeds
    hard fruit candies
    honey
    lemon juice
    buttermilk
- coffee stirrers for dipping and tasting
- sorting mat on page 121, reproduced for individual students

Science Experiments for Young Learners • EMC 866

Name _____

My Five Senses–Taste

Cut. Taste. Paste.

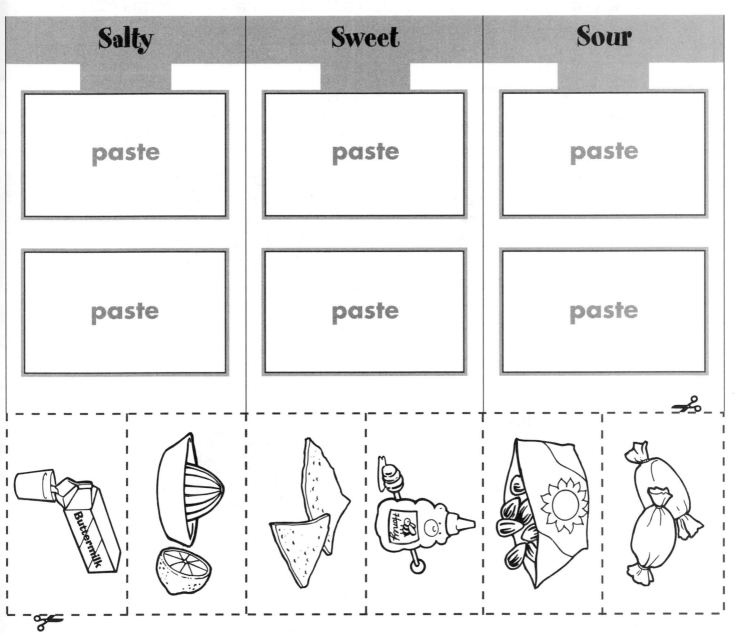

Salty	Sweet	Sour
paste	paste	paste
paste	paste	paste

Science Experiments for Young Learners • EMC 866

My Five Senses–Which Sense?

Characteristics of Organisms

Humans have senses that help them detect internal and external cues.

Students learn that we often use all our senses together to learn about something in our environment.

Doing the Experiment

1. Spread out the sheet in a large open area.

2. Put the popcorn popper in the center of the sheet. Students sit around the perimeter. (Explain that this is a scientific investigation. Students must use all their senses to describe the process of popping corn.)

3. Measure popcorn (and oil) and put it into the popper.

4. Plug in the popper and observe the popping.

5. Taste the results.

Sharing the Results

Create a class chart similar to the student record sheet. Discuss each part of the popcorn popping experience and record appropriate events under each sense.

Making Connections

Create a class "Which Sense?" chart for a different experience (a field trip, lunch hour, classroom party).

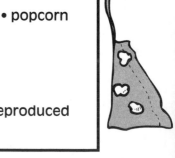

Materials

- extension cord
- popcorn
- large white sheet
- electric popcorn popper
- oil (if your popper needs it)
- record sheet on page 123, reproduced for individual students

Science Experiments for Young Learners • EMC 866

Name _____

Which Sense?

Circle the number to tell the order in which you used your senses.
Write a sentence to tell about each part of popping popcorn.

Seeing

1 2 3 4 5

Hearing

1 2 3 4 5

Tasting

1 2 3 4 5

Feeling

1 2 3 4 5

Smelling

1 2 3 4 5

Science Experiments for Young Learners • EMC 866

Growing Marigolds

Life Cycles of Organisms

Living things have a life cycle—being born, developing to adults, reproducing, and dying. Students plant marigold seeds and observe the developing plants to discover patterns in the growth cycle.

Doing the Experiment

1. Cut off the tops of the milk cartons. Poke several holes in the bottom of each carton.

2. Cover the bottom of the carton with a layer of gravel.

3. Fill the carton with potting soil. Moisten the soil with water. Press it down firmly.

4. Look at the marigold seeds carefully before planting them. Sprinkle the seeds on the surface of the soil. Scratch the surface to cover them slightly.

5. Place the carton in a sunny spot in a container to catch drips. Keep the soil moist, but not wet.

6. Wait and watch.

Sharing the Results

Watch the plants grow to maturity and then plant the new seeds. Observe the marigolds as they grow. Ask, "Do you see a pattern?"

Have students complete their record sheets.

Making Connections

Read books that describe the pattern of change plants go through. Several good choices:

Pumpkin, Pumpkin by Jeanne Titherington; Mulberry Books, 1990.

Tree of Life by Barbara Bash; Sierra Club Books, 1994.

The Seasons of Arnold's Apple Tree by Gail Gibbons; Harcourt Brace, 1988.

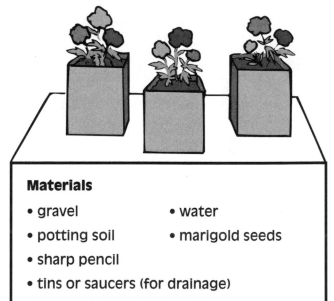

Materials
- gravel
- water
- potting soil
- marigold seeds
- sharp pencil
- tins or saucers (for drainage)
- half-pint milk cartons, clean
- record sheet on page 125, reproduced for individual students

Science Experiments for Young Learners • EMC 866

Name _____

Planting Marigolds

I planted the seed. Date planted: _____
It looked like this:

After 5 days	After 10 days	After 15 days
After 20 days	After 25 days	After 30 days

Science Experiments for Young Learners • EMC 866

Mealworm to Beetle

Life Cycles of Organisms

Living things have a life cycle—being born, developing to adults, reproducing, and dying.
Students observe mealworms as they change from larvae to pupae to adult beetles.

Doing the Experiment

1. Sprinkle a thin layer of oatmeal in the terrarium. Add several small apple chunks and damp paper towels. (Add additional oatmeal and fresh apple as needed.)

2. Add the mealworm larvae. They will eat the oatmeal and apple.

3. Watch the changes that occur as the mealworms grow and pupate. Feed the adult beetles dry dog food and vegetable bits.

4. Each day, have a student observer make a formal observation of the mealworms by completing a record sheet for the observation logbook.

Sharing the Results

Allow time for student observers to report any changes they have observed. When the mealworm's life cycle is complete, review each of the different stages.

Making Connections

Raise a butterfly in the classroom. Observe and discuss similarities and differences in life cycles.

Both mealworms and butterflies have a three-stage life cycle (complete metamorphosis).

Materials

- terrarium
- paper towels
- oatmeal, apple chunks
- box lid, spoon, hand lens
- dry dog food, vegetable bits
- mealworms (They can be inexpensively purchased at a fishing supply or pet store.)
- record sheet on page 127—reproduce one for each student. Bind together to make a class observation logbook.

Science Experiments for Young Learners • EMC 866

Name ______________________________

Life Science — My Record Sheet

Mealworm to Beetle

Date: ______________________

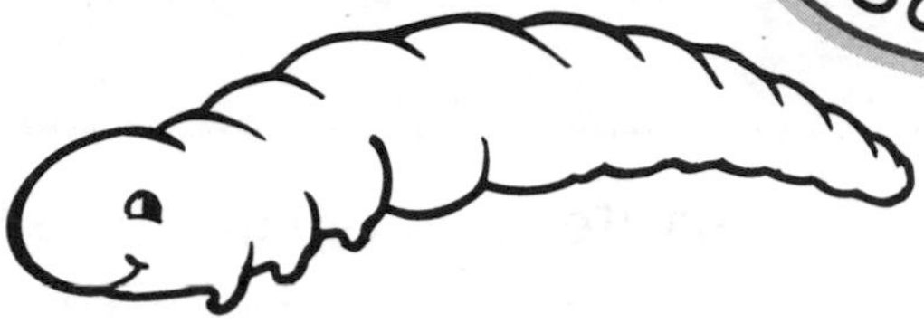

What the mealworms are doing:

____

____

____

____

Draw a mealworm here.

Animal Parents and Babies

Life Cycles of Organisms

Plants and animals closely resemble their parents.

Students match pictures to confirm that many animal young look like their parents.

Doing the Experiment

1. Give each student a set of picture cards.

2. Have students match the parents and the babies.

3. Optional: Students glue the picture pairs to a piece of construction paper.

Sharing the Results

Ask, "How were you able to match the animal parents and babies? What clues did you use?" Help students generalize that animals closely resemble their parents.

Making Connections

Have students find another parent/child animal pair and share it with the class. Students might look in library books, photo albums, magazines, or CD-ROMs.

Materials

• picture cards on page 129, reproduced for each student

• Optional: construction paper and glue

Science Experiments for Young Learners • EMC 866

Science Experiments for Young Learners • EMC 866

My Lunch Box

Organisms and Their Environments

All animals depend on plants.

Students discover our dependence on plants as a food source by analyzing the contents of a lunch box.

Doing the Experiment

1. Take out the items in the lunch box, one at a time.

2. Label the items as

   • part of a plant,
   • made from a plant, or
   • something other than a plant.

   In the case of the sandwich and the cookie, you may have to discuss ingredients in order to label the items correctly.

3. Complete the graph showing what was in the lunch box.

Sharing the Results

Discuss the lunch box graph. Then ask, "Do you eat plants?"

Making Connections

Have students complete the lunch box graph for their own lunch boxes.

Materials

• full lunch box, including:

  carrots

  lettuce

  grapes

  juice

  oatmeal cookie

  peanut butter and jelly sandwich

• graphing form on page 131, reproduced for individual students

Science Experiments for Young Learners • EMC 866

Name _____

A Lunch Box Graph

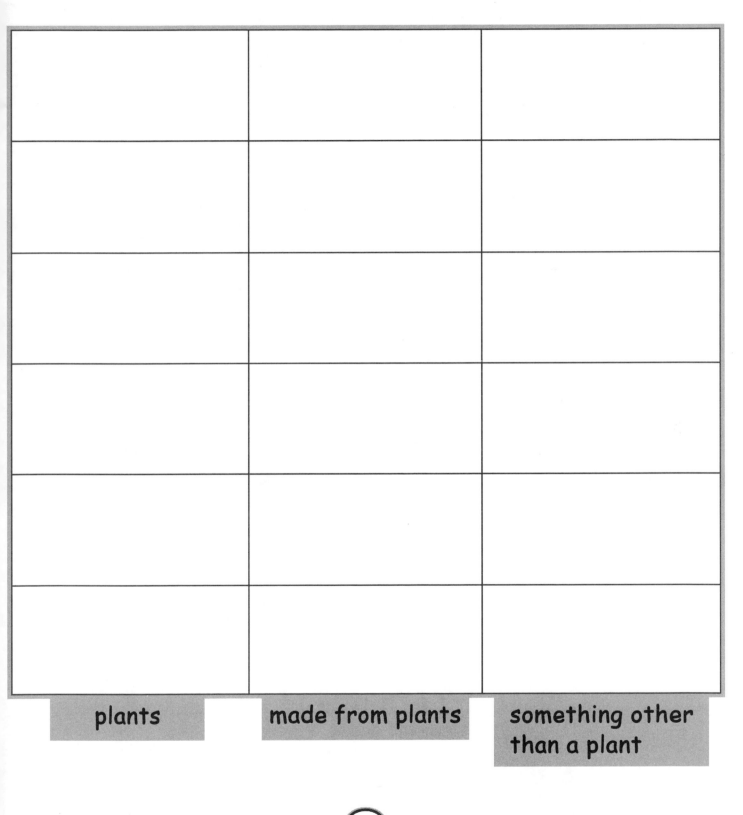

plants	made from plants	something other than a plant

Science Experiments for Young Learners • EMC 866

Plants I Use

Organisms and Their Environments

All animals depend on plants.
Students are made aware that many things we use daily are made from plants.

Doing the Experiment

1. Ask, "Does anything on the table come from plants?"

2. Lay out the labels. Students identify and sort things on the table as
   - Plants,
   - Made from Plants, or
   - Not Plants.

3. Each student finds an additional thing in the classroom that is a plant or comes from a plant and labels it or places it in the grouping on the table.

Sharing the Results

As students find classroom items that are made from plants, help them generalize that people use plants in many ways.

Making Connections

Have students locate several things in their rooms at home that are plants or made from plants.

Materials

- display a number of items, including: several types of paper, pencil, piece of cloth, cotton balls, bean seeds
- labels on page 133

Science Experiments for Young Learners • EMC 866

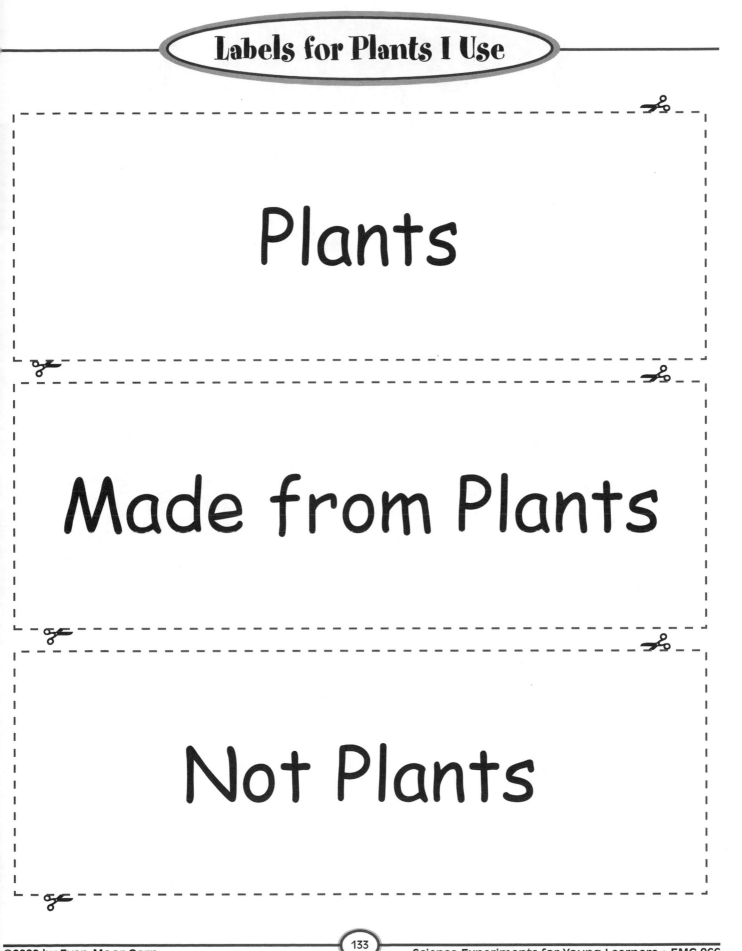

Plants

Made from Plants

Not Plants

Birdseed Plants

Organisms and Their Environments

All animals depend on plants.

Students observe that birdseed will sprout and grow into plants and conclude that birds depend on plants to live.

Doing the Experiment

1. Scoop a spoonful of birdseed onto the paper.

2. Sort the seeds into groups of the same kind. Record results on the record sheet.

3. Spoon some potting soil into each egg carton cup.

4. Label and plant the seeds. For each egg carton cup,

   • put two seeds of the same type on the sticky side of a piece of tape,

   • stick the tape on the lid of the cup, and

   • plant the other seeds of the same type in that cup.

5. Add more soil to cover the seeds.

6. Sprinkle water on the seeds.

7. Close the egg carton and place it inside the plastic bag. Tie the bag closed. Put the bag in the shade and wait for five days. Check to see if the seeds have sprouted.

8. When the seeds have sprouted, open the carton and move it into the sun.

Sharing the Results

Ask, "What happened to the birdseed? Is birdseed part of a plant? Does that mean birds eat plants?"

Making Connections

Ask, "Do you know other animals that eat plant seeds?"

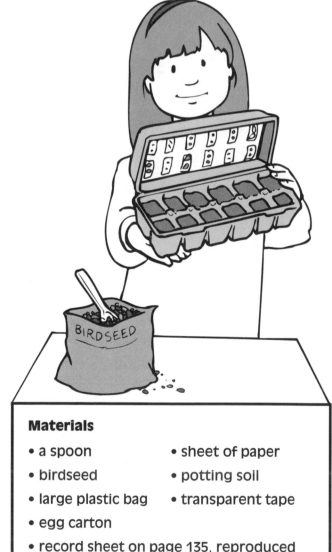

Materials

• a spoon
• birdseed
• large plastic bag
• egg carton
• record sheet on page 135, reproduced for individual students
• sheet of paper
• potting soil
• transparent tape

Science Experiments for Young Learners • EMC 866

Name _____

Birdseed Plants

My Birdseed

Draw the different kinds of seeds.

I planted the birdseed.
This is what happened.

Draw the different kinds of plants.

| Birdseed is seeds of plants. | **yes** | no |
| Birds eat plants. | **yes** | no |

A Worm Farm

Organisms cause changes in their environment.
Students observe firsthand that worms change organic waste into soil.

Doing the Experiment

1. Drill or poke holes in the bottom of the container. Make one hole every 3" to 4".

2. Set the container on bricks so that air can get into the box through the holes.

3. Tear newspaper into narrow strips. Soak the strips in water until they are soggy.

4. Put a 2" layer of soggy strips in the container.

5. Add several handfuls of soil. Mix the strips and the soil.

6. Add one pound of red worms.

7. Add scraps of food. Do not use meat or bones. Chop up broccoli stalks and an onion.

8. Cover the scraps with 2" to 3" of soggy newspaper strips.

9. Cut a rectangle from a plastic bag. Make it a little smaller than the top of your container. Put the plastic on top to keep your worm farm moist.

Sharing the Results

After a week, check your worm farm. Gently lift the newspaper and check to see if the food scraps are still there. Ask, "Where could they have gone? What happened to them?" Feed your worms again and cover them with a new layer of soggy newspaper strips. Have students complete their record sheets.

Making Connections

Send the directions for making a worm farm home to families that are interested in beginning their own worm composting service.

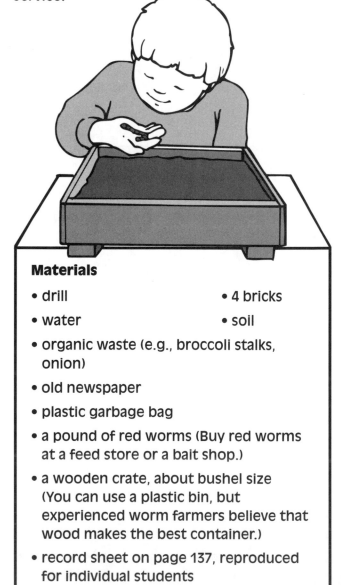

Materials

- drill
- 4 bricks
- water
- soil
- organic waste (e.g., broccoli stalks, onion)
- old newspaper
- plastic garbage bag
- a pound of red worms (Buy red worms at a feed store or a bait shop.)
- a wooden crate, about bushel size (You can use a plastic bin, but experienced worm farmers believe that wood makes the best container.)
- record sheet on page 137, reproduced for individual students

---

Science Experiments for Young Learners • EMC 866

Name _____

A Worm Farm

Label the layers of the worm farm.

paste

paste

paste

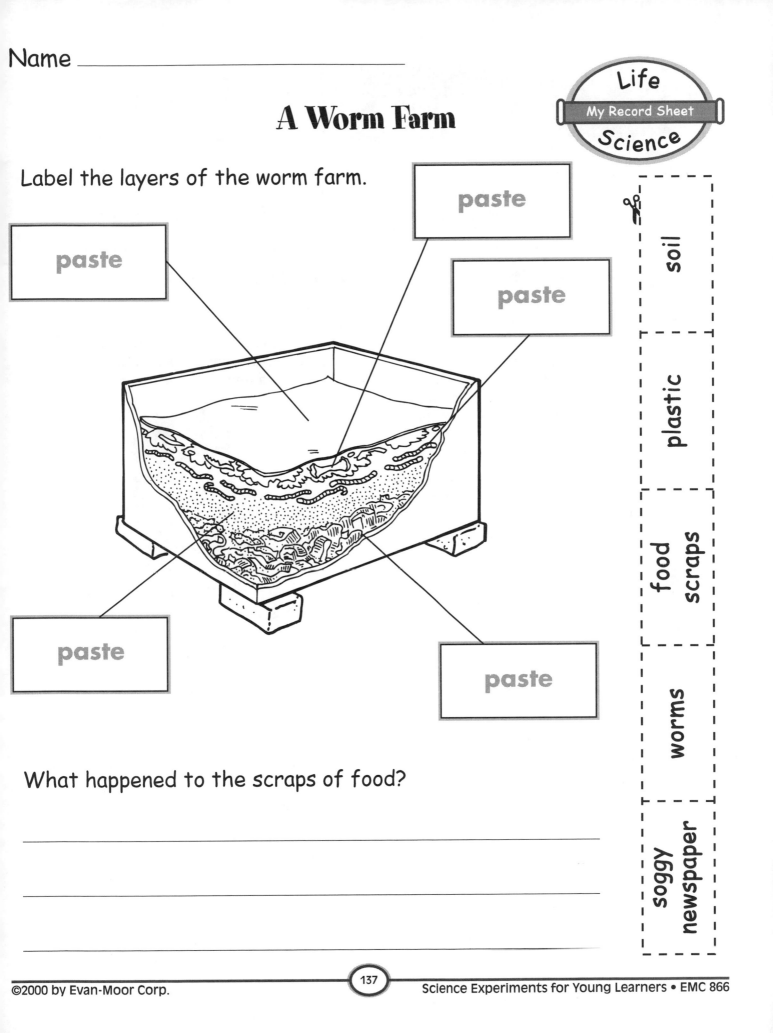

paste

paste

soil

plastic

food
scraps

worms

soggy
newspaper

What happened to the scraps of food?

_____

_____

_____

Science Experiments for Young Learners • EMC 866

A Change Survey

Organisms and Their Environments

Organisms cause changes in their environment.

Students observe a single spot over time and conclude that people and animals change their environment.

Doing the Experiment

1. Choose a spot for the observation. Depending on the level of your students, observe one spot as a class or assign individual spots to individual students. (The spot(s) can be indoors, although this experiment assumes it is outdoors.) Mark the spot in some way so students will be able to return to the same spot several times during the next week.

2. Discuss the kinds of changes students might observe. For example, a spot on the asphalt may have chalk drawings on it, grass may be shorter or wetter, or an insect may build a home.

3. Students sit quietly and note in their logs what they see at their spot.

4. Students return to their spots on subsequent days to note changes.

Sharing the Results

Students share their observation logs with classmates. List any changes that students have observed. Then ask, "What caused the changes?" Help students generalize that living things can change their environment.

Making Connections

Play "How Could You Change It?" One student names a place or thing. Others think of ways they could change it (e.g., *the playground—I could build a new swing. I could plant a tree.*).

Materials

- a designated spot
- change log on page 139, reproduced for individual students

My Change Log

_____

Name

Day 1

Day 2

Day 3

Day 4

Day 5

Drip a Gallon

Organisms and Their Environments

Organisms cause changes in their environment.

Students observe that even a slowly dripping faucet can result in substantial waste of a valuable resource.

Doing the Experiment

1. Have students estimate how long it will take to drip a gallon of water.

2. Turn on the faucet so that there is a slow drip.

3. Put the gallon container under the classroom faucet.

4. Watch to see when it is full. Record water levels at specified times on the record sheets.

Sharing the Results

Compare student estimates with the actual results.

Making Connections

Discuss the importance of conserving water. Have students count the number of faucets in the school. Ask, "What would happen if each of the faucets leaked?"

Materials

- faucet
- clock
- gallon container
- record sheet on page 141, reproduced for individual students

Science Experiments for Young Learners • EMC 866

Drip a Gallon

Make a line to show how full the container is.

Key

- Use **blue** after 30 minutes.
- Use **green** after 2 hours.
- Use **red** after 3 hours.
- Use **brown** after 6 hours.

Science Experiments for Young Learners • EMC 866

Name _____

Life
My Log
Science

_____

_____

_____

_____

_____

_____

_____

_____

©2000 by Evan-Moor Corp.　　　　Science Experiments for Young Learners • EMC 866

Earth and Space Science

- Materials have different physical properties that make them useful in different ways.

- Water has different physical properties.

- Water has different physical and chemical properties.

- The properties of materials make them useful.

- Air has different physical and chemical properties.

- Rocks have different physical properties.

- Soil has different physical properties.

- Soils have varied abilities to support plant growth.

- Earth materials have different physical properties.

- Fossils provide evidence of life long ago.

- The sun, moon, stars, and clouds have properties that can be observed.

- The sun provides light and heat.

- The surface of the earth changes.

- Weather can be described by measurable quantities.

- Weather changes from day to day.

- Objects in the sky have patterns of movement.

Science Experiments for Young Learners • EMC 866

Will It Float?

Properties of Earth Materials

Materials have different physical properties that make them useful in different ways.
Students experiment to find out which objects will sink and which will float.

Doing the Experiment

1. Students predict which objects will float, and mark predictions on the record sheet.

2. Students put each object in the tub of water to see if it will sink or float.

3. Students record the results on the record sheet.

Sharing the Results

Students share their discoveries. Group the actual objects into a floating group and a sinking group. Ask, "Do the groups have distinctive characteristics?"

Making Connections

Ask, "Can you think of something else that will float? sink? Why might it be important to know if something will sink or float?"

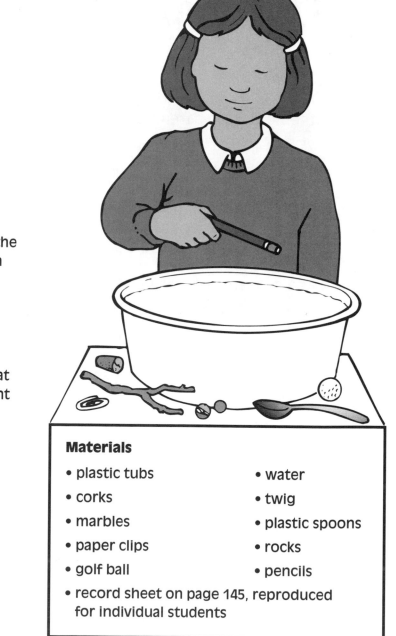

Materials

- plastic tubs
- corks
- marbles
- paper clips
- golf ball
- water
- twig
- plastic spoons
- rocks
- pencils
- record sheet on page 145, reproduced for individual students

Science Experiments for Young Learners • EMC 866

Name _____

Will It Float?

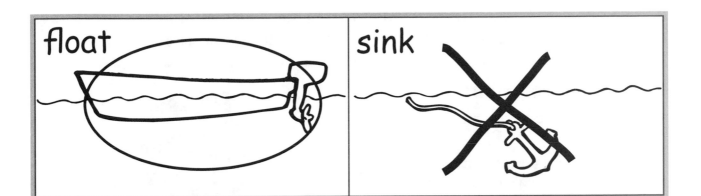

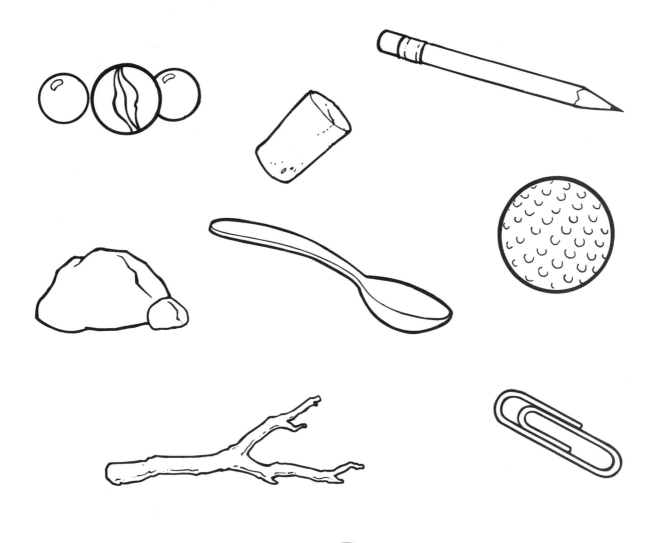

©2000 by Evan-Moor Corp.

Science Experiments for Young Learners • EMC 866

Make It Float

Properties of Earth Materials

Materials have different physical properties that make them useful in different ways.
Students discover how to make a lump of clay float by changing its shape.

Doing the Experiment

1. Drop the lump of clay into the water. Watch it sink.

2. Give each student a lump of clay. Challenge them to change the shape of the clay so that it will float. Students must use the entire lump of clay so that the only thing they are changing is the shape.

3. Test floaters to see if they float.

4. Students draw shapes and record test results on their record sheets.

Sharing the Results

Have students show their clay "floaters." Group the floaters into those that did float and those that did not float. Ask, "What is the same about those that float?"

Floating is determined by how much water an object pushes out of the way, or displaces. Objects that displace lots of water receive a strong upward push from the water underneath. This push can support the object and allows it to float.

Materials

- large tub of water
- fist-sized lumps of modeling clay (one per student)
- record sheet on page 147, reproduced for individual students

Making Connections

Ask, "How does changing your shape when you're in the swimming pool help you float?"

Science Experiments for Young Learners • EMC 866

Name _____

Floating Clay

This is my clay.

When I put it in the water, this is what happened.

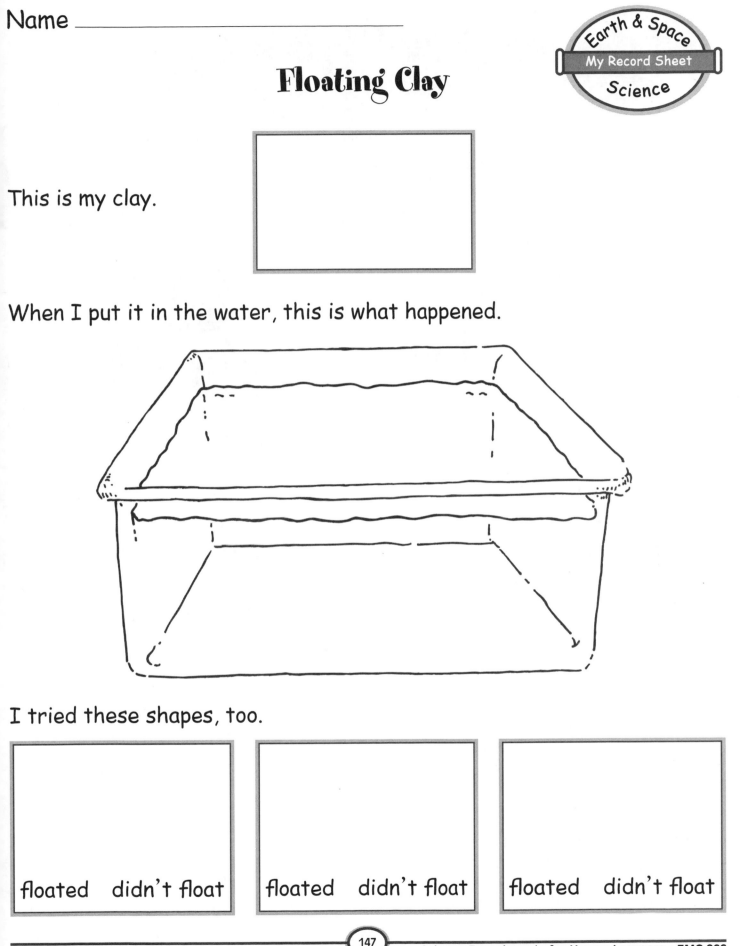

I tried these shapes, too.

floated didn't float	floated didn't float	floated didn't float

Float a Paper Clip

Properties of Earth Materials

Water has different physical properties.

Students discover that water has a "skin."

Doing the Experiment

1. Fill the bowl with water.

2. Drop the paper clip into the water. (It will sink.)

3. Remove the paper clip from the water and dry it. Students record the results of this attempt on their record sheets.

4. Set the paper clip on the tines of a fork. Slowly lower the fork until the clip rests on the water's surface.

5. Gently remove the fork, and the clip will float. Students record the results on their record sheets.

Sharing the Results

Ask, "Why did the paper clip float? What was different the second time?"

Primary students can think of the surface molecules as muscle-man molecules. They "hold hands very tightly" so the water molecules below can't break through. The strong bond between these water molecules along the surface forms a "skin." This skin is called surface tension.

Materials

- plastic bowl
- fork
- paper clip
- water
- record sheet on page 149, reproduced for individual students

Making Connections

Ask students to tell how a water bug that strides across a pond is like the paper clip.

Science Experiments for Young Learners • EMC 866

Name _____

Float a Paper Clip

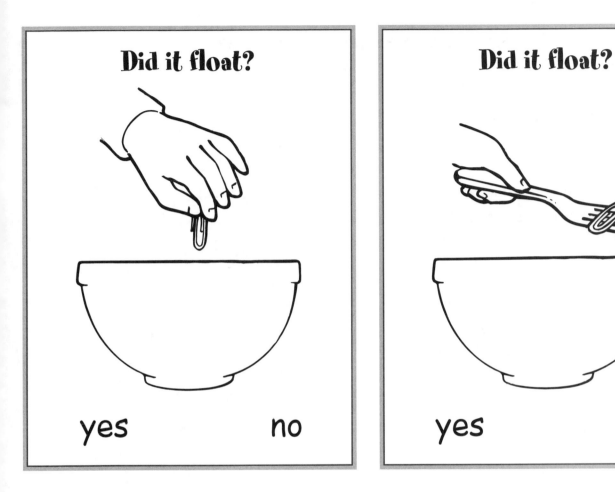

Did it float?	Did it float?
yes no	yes no

Why did it float?

_____

_____

_____

_____

Strong Water

Properties of Earth Materials

Water has different physical properties.
Students discover that surface tension allows water to rise above the rim of a container.

Doing the Experiment

1. Fill the bowl all the way to the top with water.

2. Slowly slide a penny into the water.

3. Continue to add pennies one at a time. Count how many you add. Record the number on the record sheet.

Sharing the Results

Ask, "How many pennies were added before the water overflowed? What did you notice about the surface of the water?"

Just before the water overflows, you will be able to see how the surface tension pulls the surface of the water together so it curves above the rim of the container.

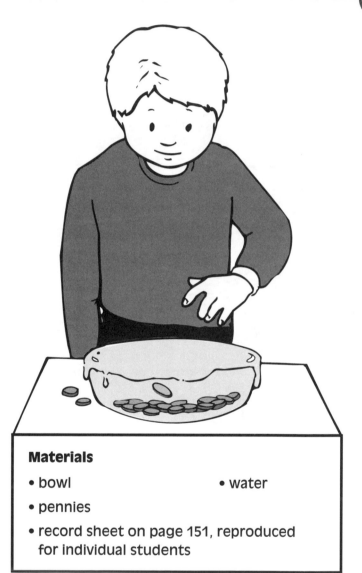

Making Connections

Ask students if they have ever seen a drip forming on a faucet. The drip bulges out of the faucet before it falls. Ask, "What makes the drip bulge?"

Materials

- bowl
- pennies
- record sheet on page 151, reproduced for individual students
- water

Science Experiments for Young Learners • EMC 866

Name _____

Strong Water

Earth & Space
My Record Sheet
Science

Draw the water in the bowl.

This is my bowl.

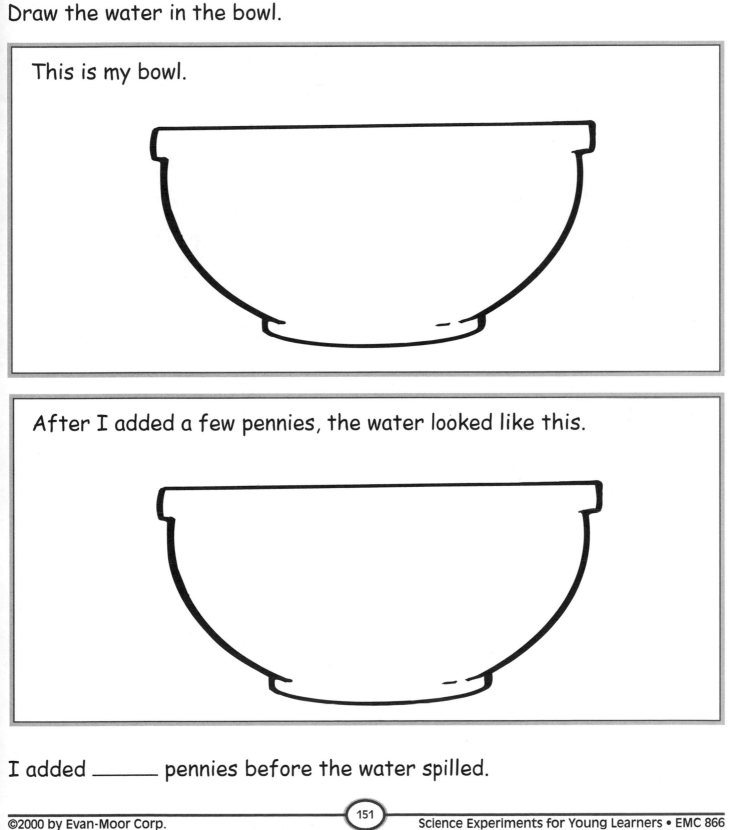

After I added a few pennies, the water looked like this.

I added _____ pennies before the water spilled.

Science Experiments for Young Learners • EMC 866

Drop It!

Properties of Earth Materials

Water has different physical properties.
Students investigate to discover the shape of water drops.

Doing the Experiment

Note: Before you begin the experiment, demonstrate the use of an eyedropper to drop water onto the square of waxed paper.

1. Investigate the shape of a drop.

   • Put one drop of water on the square.

   • Look at the drop from the side.

2. Draw what you see.

3. Repeat the investigation several times. Check to see if the shape is the same each time. Have students complete their record sheets.

Sharing the Results

Students report on what they found out about the water drops. Have them vote to indicate the shape they saw.

Making Connections

Ask students if they have seen other drops of water (drops that form on the hood of a car early in the morning, dew on the grass, drips on a counter). Ask, "What shape are the drops? Does the shape of the drop have anything to do with surface tension?"

Materials

• for each student:
   eyedropper
   water
   paper towel or newspaper
   small square of waxed paper

• record sheet on page 153, reproduced for individual students

Science Experiments for Young Learners • EMC 866

Name _____

Drop It!

Draw a side view of your drop. Circle the shape you think it is most like.

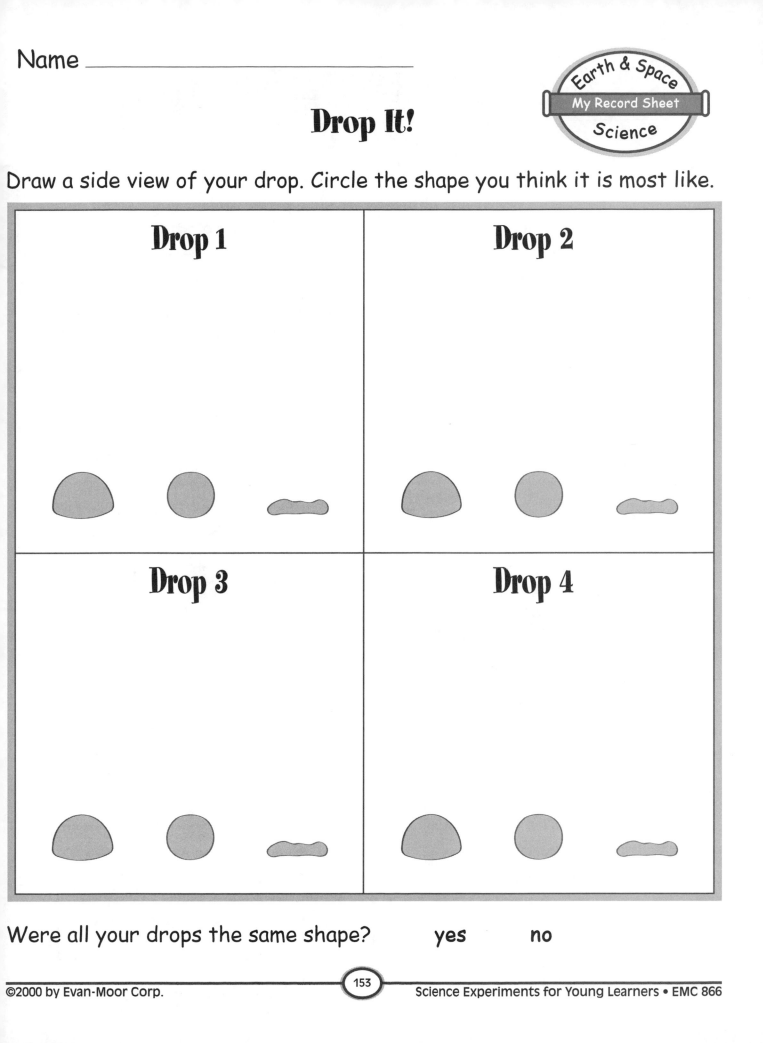

Drop 1

Drop 2

Drop 3

Drop 4

Were all your drops the same shape?   yes   no

Science Experiments for Young Learners • EMC 866

Surface Tension and Soap

Properties of Earth Materials

Water has different physical properties.
Students learn that soap weakens the surface tension of water.

Doing the Experiment

1. Fill the bowl with water.

2. Sprinkle pepper on top.

3. Drop a single drop of detergent into the center of the bowl.

4. Watch what happens. Record results on the record sheet.

Sharing the Results

Have students describe what they saw. Ask, "Why was the pepper floating on top of the water? What happened when the detergent was added?"

The soap molecules weaken the surface tension in the center of the bowl. The stronger surface tension around the edge of the bowl pulls the pepper outward.

Making Connections

Try blowing a bubble with regular water. Try blowing a bubble with soapy solution. Ask, "Why can you blow a bubble with the soap solution?"

Carefully drop a handkerchief into a tub of clean water. The handkerchief will float. Add a few drops of detergent. Ask, "What happens when the detergent is added?"

(The soap reduces the surface tension and the handkerchief sinks.) If you have done *Float a Paper Clip* (page 148), repeat the experiment. Add a few drops of detergent to the bowl where the paper clip is floating. Ask, "What made the surface tension change?"

Materials

- bowl or pie pan
- water
- ground pepper
- liquid detergent
- record sheet on page 155, reproduced for individual students

Science Experiments for Young Learners • EMC 866

Surface Tension and Soap

Draw the pepper.

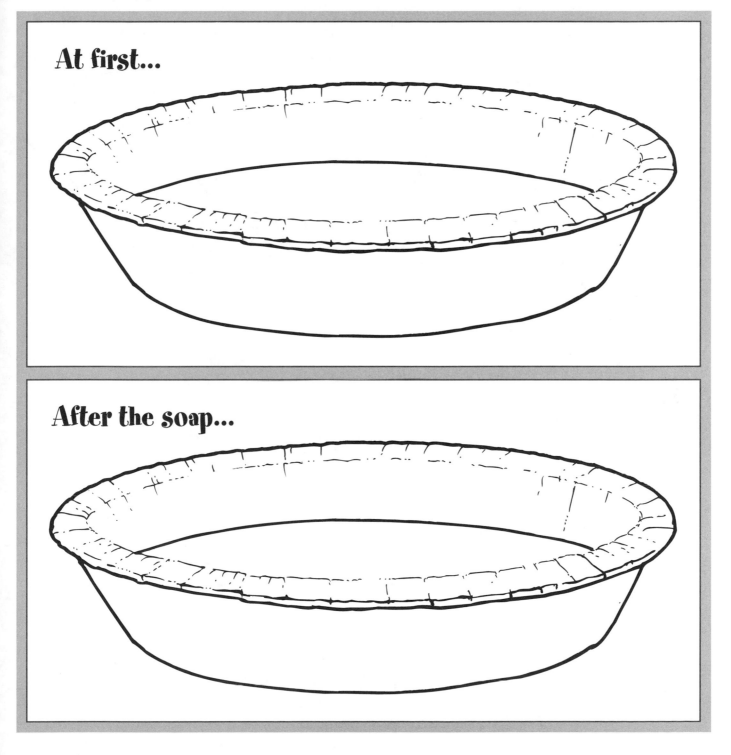

At first...

After the soap...

Frozen Water

Properties of Earth Materials

Water has different physical and chemical properties.
Students experiment to discover that water expands when it freezes.

Doing the Experiment

1. Each student fills a glass about half full of water.

2. Mark the levels with a piece of masking tape. Write names on the tape to identify glasses.

3. Record the level of the water on the record sheet.

4. Put the glasses in the freezer overnight.

5. Remove the frozen water from the freezer. Compare the level of the ice with the tape that shows the previous water level.

6. Record the results on the record sheet.

Sharing the Results

Ask, "Did the water change? Did the water stay the same size, get smaller, or get bigger when it turned into ice?"

When water freezes it takes up more space.

Making Connections

Try freezing other liquids to see if they also take up more space when frozen (juice, milk, soup).

There's more ice than there was water!

Peter   Carlos

Materials

- water
- masking tape
- clear plastic glasses
- access to a freezer
- record sheet on page 157, reproduced for individual students

Science Experiments for Young Learners • EMC 866

Name _____

Frozen Water

Water   **Frozen Water**

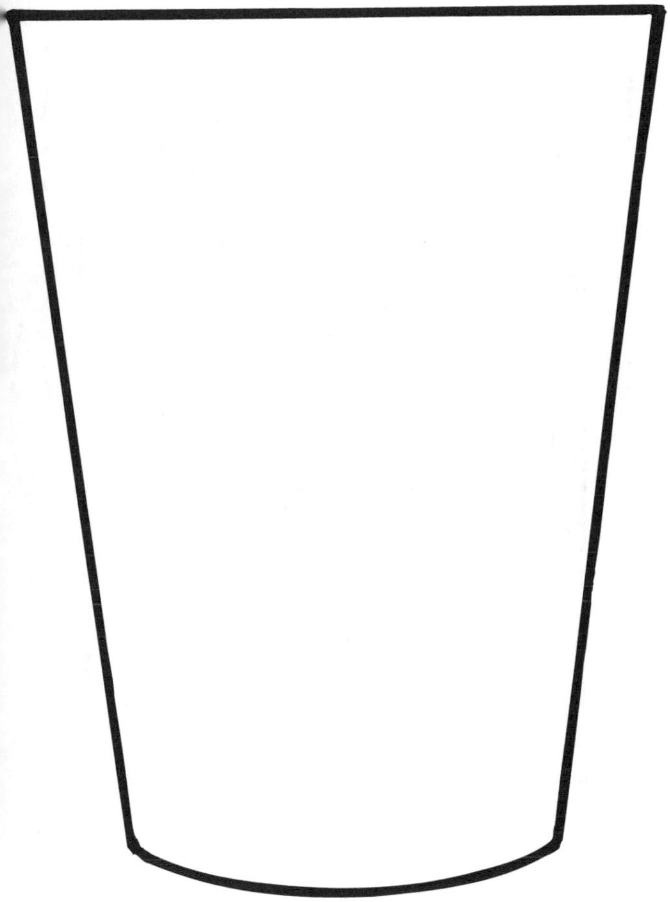

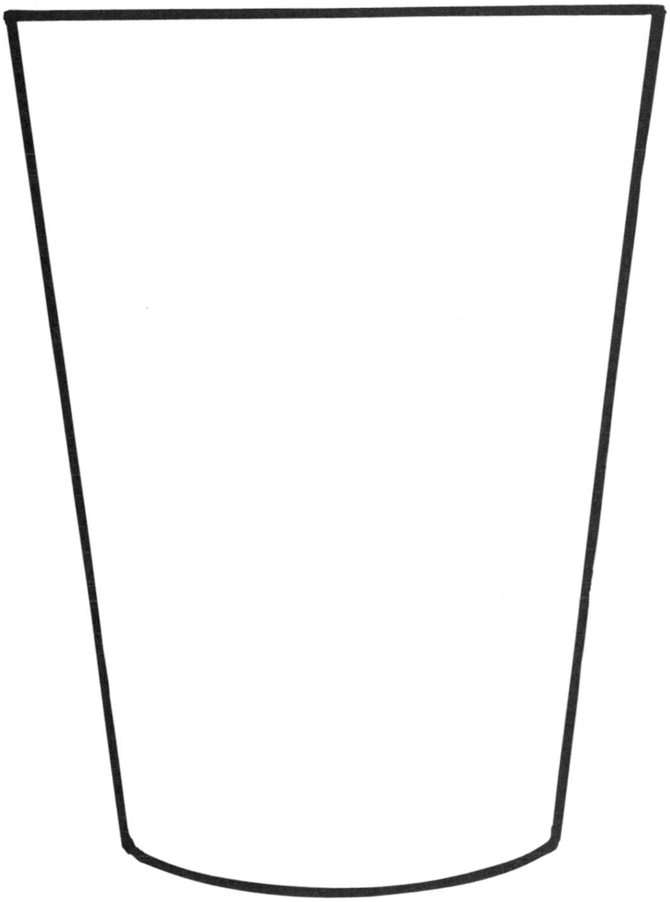

Write to tell what happened.

_____

_____

_____

Science Experiments for Young Learners • EMC 866

Raise the Lid

Properties of Earth Materials

Water has different physical and chemical properties.

Students observe that freezing water exerts a force when it expands.

Doing the Experiment

1. Fill the bottle to the brim with water. Note level of water on the record sheet.

2. Cover the bottle with a loose-fitting cap made of aluminum foil.

3. Put the bottle in the freezer. Leave it until the water has frozen solid.

4. Observe what happens to the aluminum foil cap. Record results on the record sheet.

Sharing the Results

Ask students to explain why the foil cap was pushed up.

Ice takes up more space than the water that froze.

Making Connections

Ask, "What would happen to pipes if they froze when they were full of water?" *(The water inside the pipes will expand as it freezes. It may force the pipe joints apart or make the pipes split.)*

Materials

- water
- freezer
- a small bottle made of glass or thick plastic (a food coloring bottle works well)
- square of aluminum foil
- record sheet on page 159, reproduced for individual students

Science Experiments for Young Learners • EMC 866

Name _____

Raise the Lid

Draw the aluminum cap on each bottle.

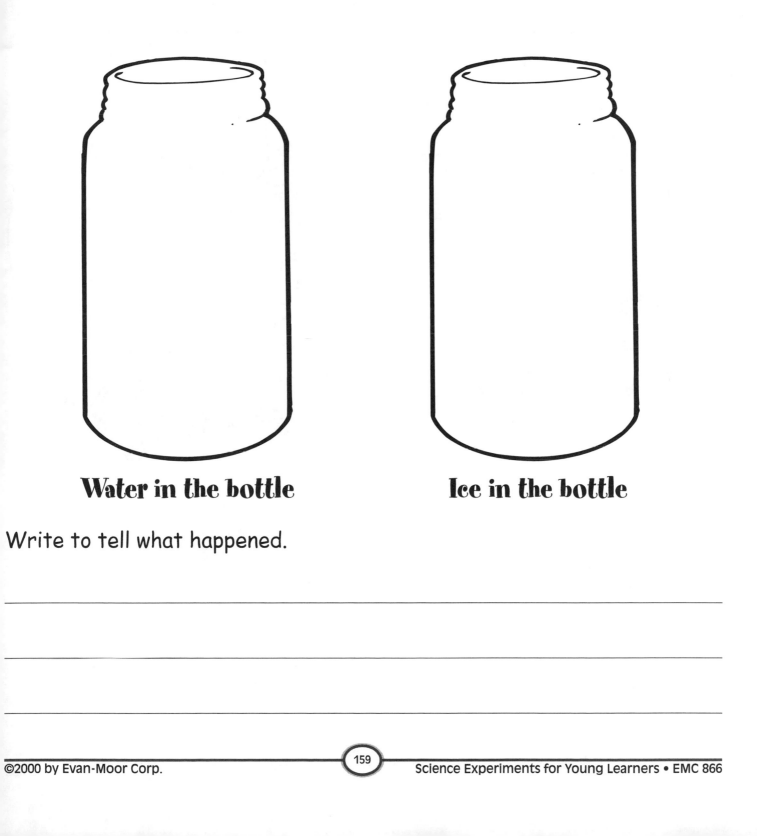

Water in the bottle   **Ice in the bottle**

Write to tell what happened.

_____

_____

_____

Flowing Water

Properties of Earth Materials

Water has different physical properties.
Students discover that water flows downhill.

Doing the Experiment

1. Have children work in small groups. Each group uses wooden blocks to raise one end of a washtub.

2. Groups pour water into the tubs at the high end and observe the flow.

3. Students record results on the record sheet by drawing the flow with a blue crayon.

4. Challenge students to raise and lower the tub to try to see if the water will flow uphill and remain there.

Sharing the Results

Ask, "Which way did the water move? Why do you think water always moves downward?"

Gravity causes water to flow downhill.

Making Connections

Encourage students to build hills and moats in the sand area. Supply water and ask students to observe the downhill flow.

Materials

• containers of water

• rectangular washtubs

• large wooden blocks

• blue crayons

• sponges and paper towels for spills

• record sheet on page 161, reproduced for individual students

Science Experiments for Young Learners • EMC 866

Name _____

Flowing Water

Use your blue crayon to show how the water flows.

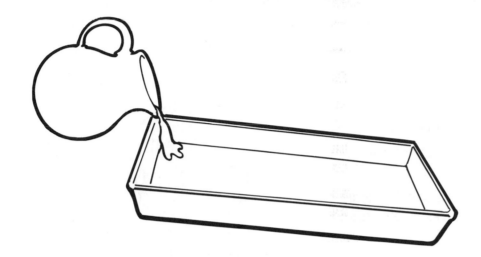

What do you think will happen?

Science Experiments for Young Learners • EMC 866

Working Water

Properties of Earth Materials

The properties of materials make them useful.
Students experiment to find out that moving water can move things.

Doing the Experiment

1. Make a waterwheel.

   - Cut out the waterwheel pattern.

   - Fold each section over to form a "cup" to catch the water.

   - Push the wheel onto a pencil. Wiggle the wheel until it moves freely around the pencil.

2. Hold the wheel under moving water from a faucet or container. (Be sure the cup sections are pointing up.)

3. Watch the water turn the wheel.

Sharing the Results

Ask, "Did your waterwheel turn? What made the wheel turn?"

Making Connections

Ask, "Have you ever seen moving water at work?" *(paddle boats, mills, dams)*

Materials

- pencils   • water
- plastic washtubs or sink
- waterwheel pattern on page 163, reproduced on tagboard for individual students

Science Experiments for Young Learners • EMC 866

Waterwheel Pattern

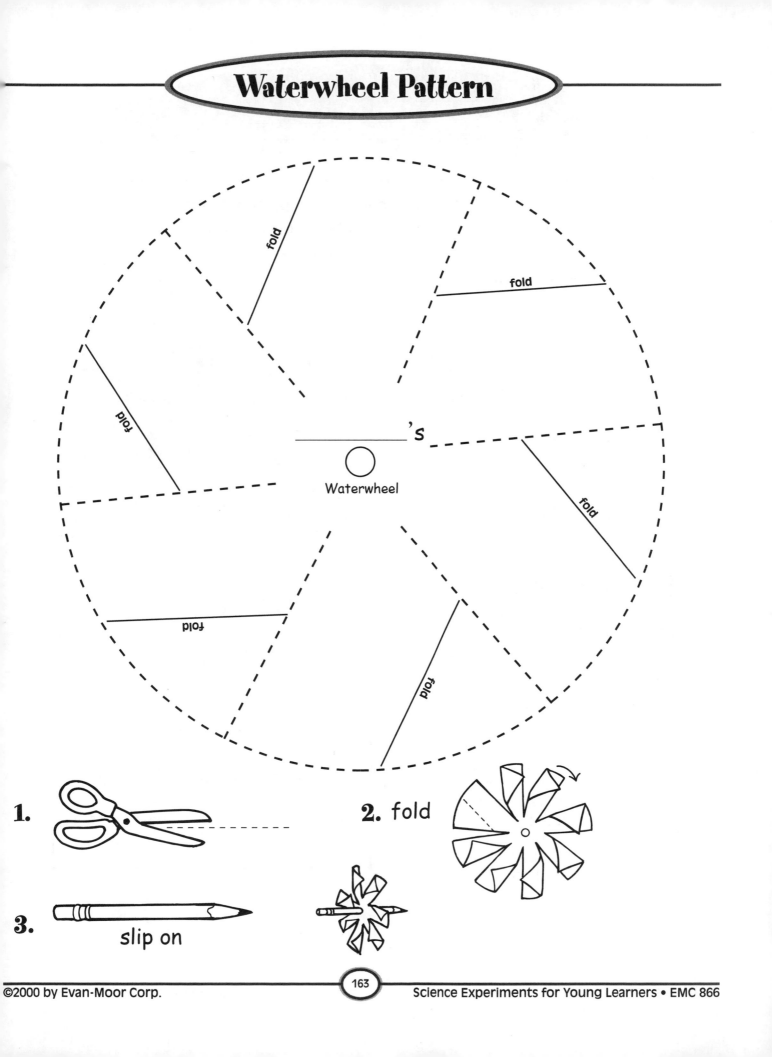

fold

fold

fold

fold

fold

fold

_____'s

Waterwheel

1.

2. fold

3. slip on

Science Experiments for Young Learners • EMC 866

Air Is Everywhere

Properties of Earth Materials

Air has different physical and chemical properties.
Students confirm that, although invisible, there is air all around.

Doing the Experiment

1. Show the closed plastic bag. Have students guess what's inside the bag.

2. Have one child hold out an arm. Open the bag, pressing so that the rush of air can be felt. Ask the student to describe what he or she felt.

3. Ask students again what is in the bag. Take suggestions. If the students don't guess the correct answer, explain that the bag was full of air.

4. Have students draw three things in the classroom that are filled with air.

Sharing the Results

Students share their drawings and discuss what they know about air.

Making Connections

Have students bring a container of air from home. Discuss how air might be collected and how it can be held while bringing it to school. When students bring in containers, label them and display them. Ask, "How is the air in the containers alike or different?" Open the containers and release the air. Ask, "Is the air different in appearance, feel, or smell? Could the air be recaptured?" Have students take "school air" home in their containers.

Materials

- large self-closing bag, closed with air inside
- record sheet on page 165, reproduced for individual students

Science Experiments for Young Learners • EMC 866

Name _____

Air in the Classroom

Where could air be?
Draw three things in the classroom that are filled with air.

Science Experiments for Young Learners • EMC 866

The Magic Glass

Properties of Earth Materials

Air has different physical and chemical properties.
Students confirm that, although invisible, air is all around.

Doing the Experiment

1. Fill the big bowl with water. Note: Water must be deeper than the height of the glass. Add food coloring.

2. Hold an empty glass upside down. Press it down into the water. (Make sure the glass is straight up and down.)

3. Look at the glass through the water. (The water does not fill the glass.)

4. Record observations on the record sheet.

Sharing the Results

Students share ideas about why the glass doesn't fill with water.

Making Connections

Repeat the experiment. This time, after you have pressed the glass into the water, tip it so bubbles of air can escape. Ask students to explain what the bubbles prove.

Materials

- water
- food coloring
- clear glass
- big bowl or fish tank
- record sheet on page 167, reproduced for individual students

Science Experiments for Young Learners • EMC 866

Name _____

The Magic Glass

Draw the water.

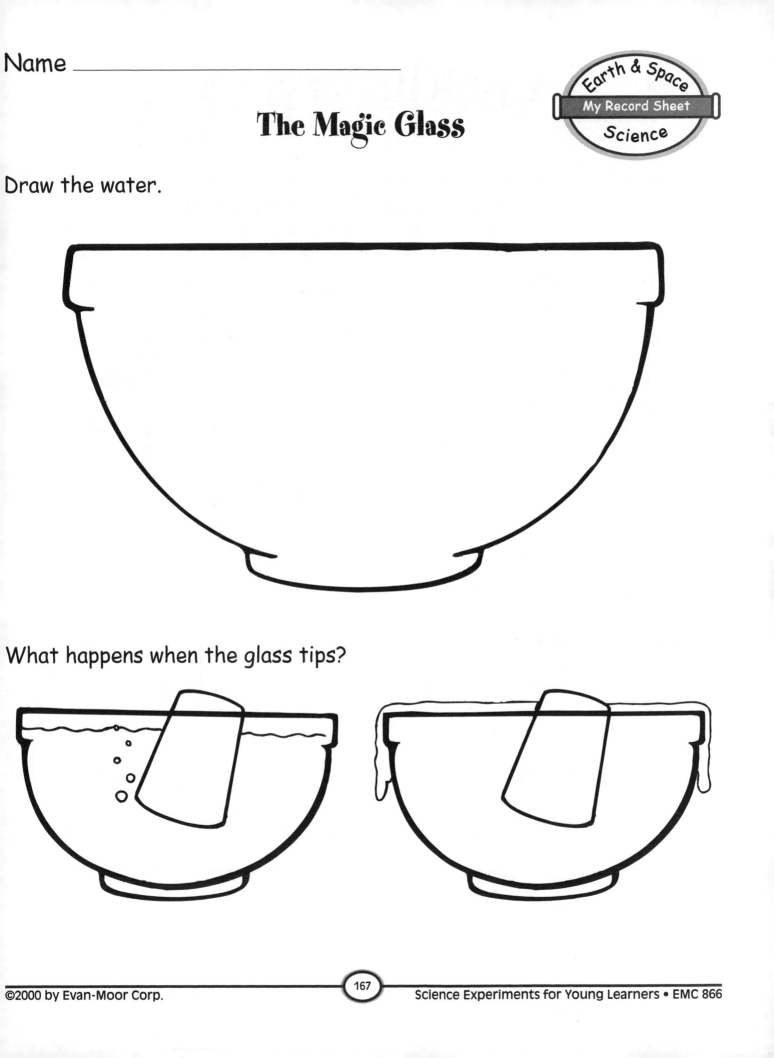

What happens when the glass tips?

©2000 by Evan-Moor Corp.   Science Experiments for Young Learners • EMC 866

The Mysterious Funnel

Properties of Earth Materials

Air has different physical and chemical properties.

Students observe that air takes up space.

Doing the Experiment

1. Put the funnel in the neck of the bottle.

2. Seal the gap between the funnel and the mouth of the bottle with modeling clay.

3. Pour some water into the funnel.

4. Have students observe and record what they see.

5. Use the knitting needle to make a small hole in the clay.

6. Note what happens and record the results on the record sheet.

Sharing the Results

Ask, "Why didn't the water go into the bottle at first? What caused the change?"

The bottle is full of air. The modeling clay stopped the air from escaping. When a hole is made in the clay, the air is able to get out of the bottle so the water rushes in to fill the space.

Making Connections

Bring a large plastic container of water that has a spigot. Do not make the air hole in the top of the container, and then open the spigot. The water will flow out only briefly. Make the hole and note the change. Relate the air hole to the hole in the clay in the Mysterious Funnel.

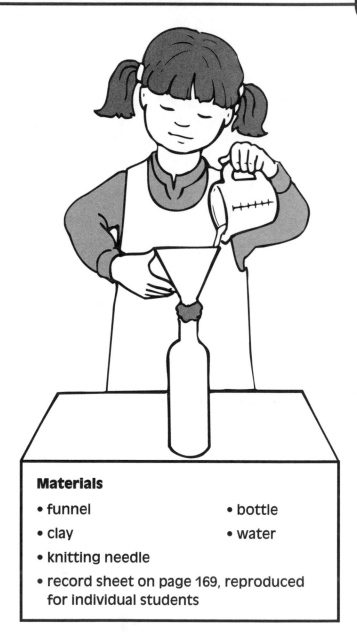

Materials

- funnel
- clay
- knitting needle
- record sheet on page 169, reproduced for individual students
- bottle
- water

Science Experiments for Young Learners • EMC 866

Name _____

The Mysterious Funnel

Draw the water to show what happened.

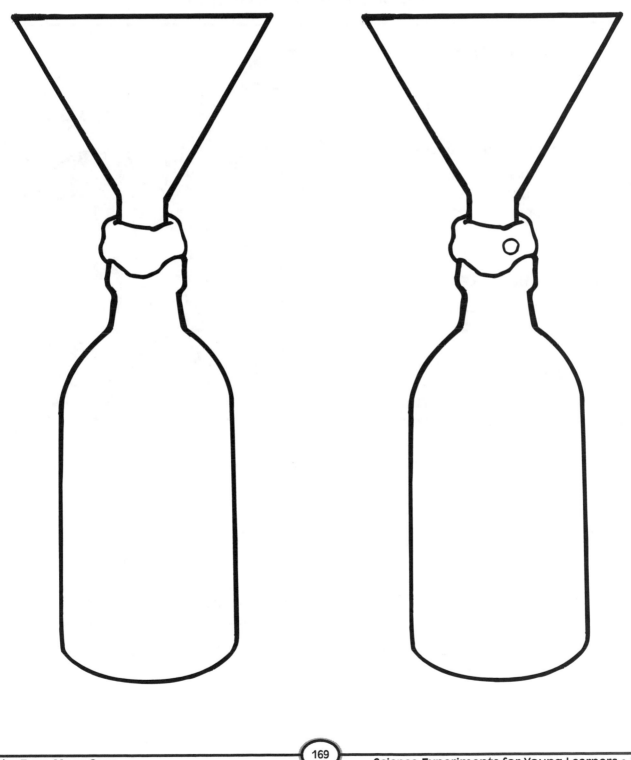

Fill It Up!

Air has different physical and chemical properties.

Students observe that air takes up space.

Doing the Experiment

1. Look at a paper lunch bag.

2. Blow into the bag. Hold the top tight with your hands.

3. Observe and record the changes.

4. In a similar manner, blow air into a balloon and a beach ball. Have students complete their activity sheets.

Sharing the Results

Students confirm that when air is put inside something it takes up space.

Making Connections

Have students put their hands on their chests and breathe deeply. Explain that the air they breathe in is filling their lungs in about the same way that the lunch bags, the balloon, and the beach ball were filled with air. Ask students to name other examples (*pumping up a tire, inflating a raft, filling an air mattress*).

Materials

- balloon
- paper lunch bags
- deflated beach ball
- activity sheet on page 171, reproduced for individual students

Name _____

Fill It Up!

Cut and paste to show **no air** and **full of air**.

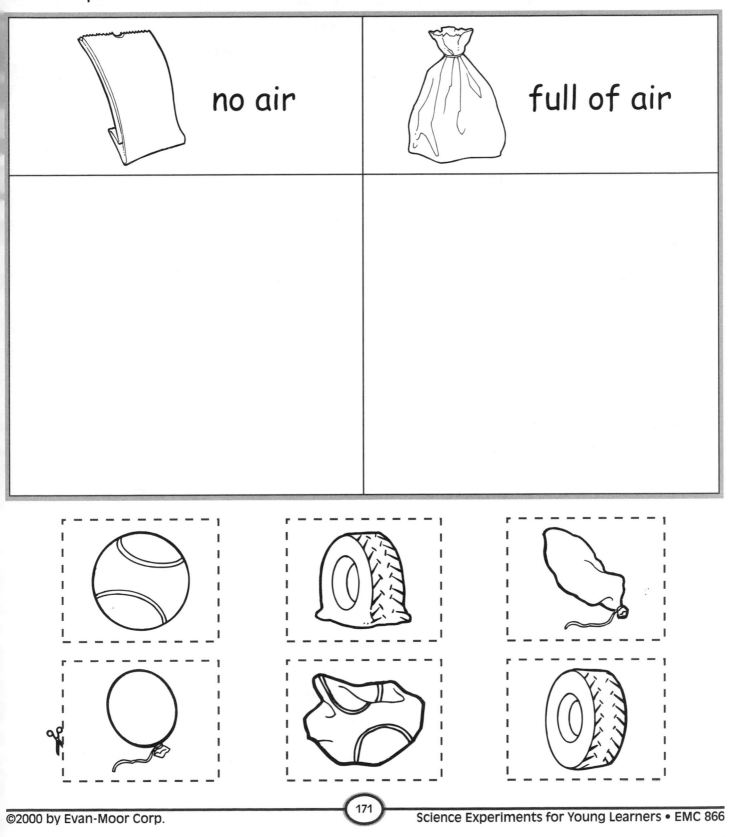

no air

full of air

Changing Shape

Properties of Earth Materials

Air has different physical and chemical properties.
Students observe that air takes the shape of the container it fills.

Doing the Experiment

1. Fill the fish tank with water.

2. Put one glass bottom down into the tank. The glass will fill with water.

3. Push the second glass into the water mouth down.

4. Ask, "What is keeping the water out of the glass? What shape is the air in the second glass?" Have students record their observations on their record sheets (Observation 1).

5. Holding the second glass still, pick up the first glass. Turn it over while still under the water. Hold it upside down just to the side of the second glass.

6. Tilt the air-filled glass (first glass) to allow air bubbles to escape. Catch the bubbles in the other glass as shown in the illustration. (The air bubbles will push the water out of the glass and take its shape.)

7. Students record the change on their record sheets (Observation 2).

Sharing the Results

Have students describe how the air changed shape.

> *Air has no shape of its own. It takes the shape of the container it fills.*

Making Connections

Discuss the shape of air in containers in your classroom. Students can draw a container and then trace the drawing to show the shape that the air inside the container would have.

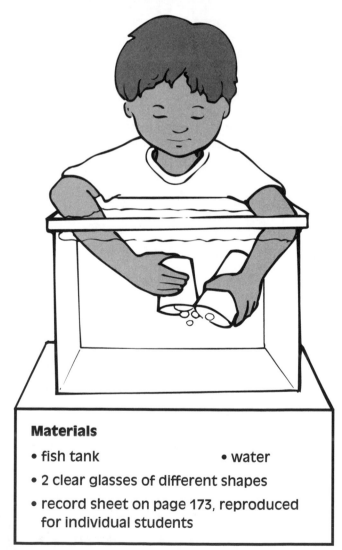

Materials
- fish tank
- water
- 2 clear glasses of different shapes
- record sheet on page 173, reproduced for individual students

Science Experiments for Young Learners • EMC 866

Name _____

Changing Shape

Earth & Space
My Record Sheet
Science

Draw the glasses in the tank. Color the water blue.	Draw the glasses in the tank. Color the water blue.
Observation 1	**Observation 2**

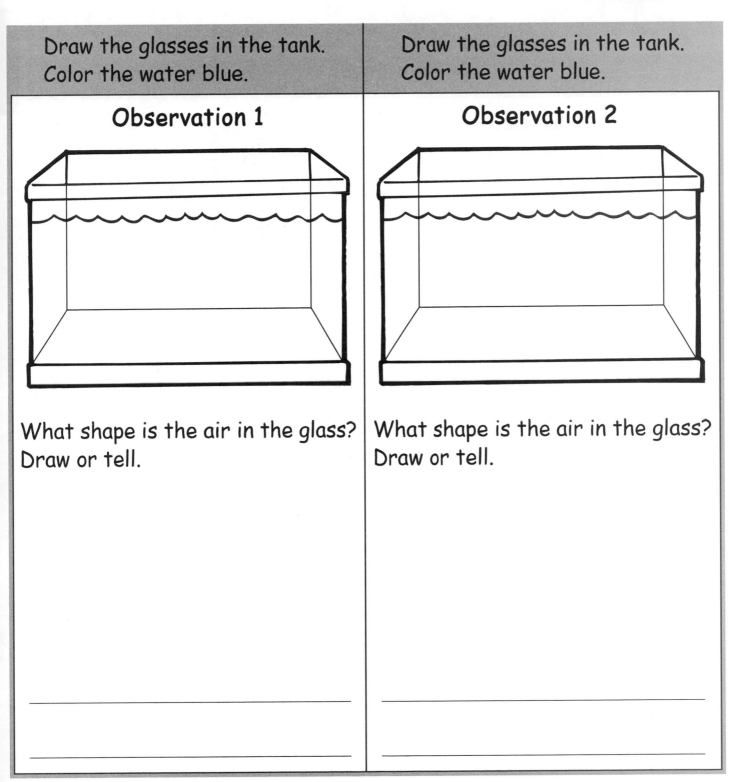

What shape is the air in the glass? Draw or tell.

_____

_____

What shape is the air in the glass? Draw or tell.

_____

_____

Science Experiments for Young Learners • EMC 866

Which Weighs More?

Air has different physical and chemical properties.
Students discover that air has weight.

Doing the Experiment

1. Put the deflated playground ball on one side of a balance.

2. Count as you place counters on the other side of the scale until it balances.

3. Pump the ball full of air with an air pump.

4. Weigh the ball again.

Sharing the Results

Ask, "What happened? What was changed? Why did the ball weigh more the second time?" Apply the observation that air has weight by completing the activity sheet.

Making Connections

Ask your students how much they think the air in your classroom weighs.

While air is a very light substance, the air in an average classroom weighs about 150 pounds.

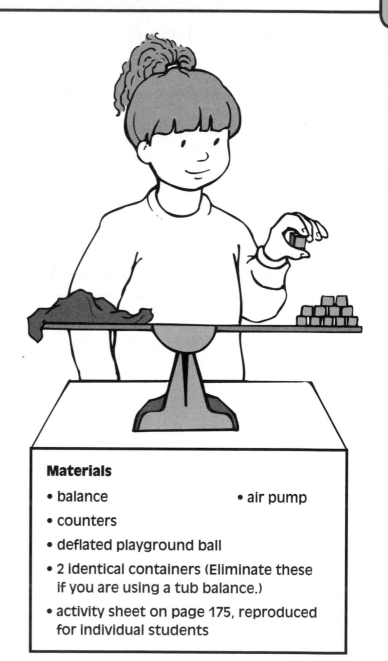

Materials

- balance
- air pump
- counters
- deflated playground ball
- 2 identical containers (Eliminate these if you are using a tub balance.)
- activity sheet on page 175, reproduced for individual students

Science Experiments for Young Learners • EMC 866

Name _____

Which Weighs More?

Mark the object in each pair that weighs more.

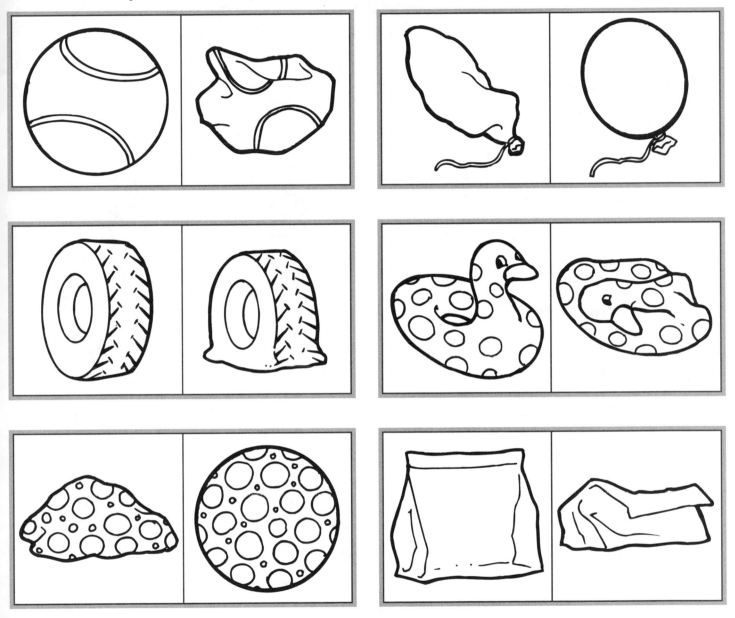

Why do the ones you marked weigh more?

_____

_____

©2000 by Evan-Moor Corp.   Science Experiments for Young Learners • EMC 866

Spinning Spiral

Properties of Earth Materials

Air has different physical and chemical properties.
Students experiment and conclude that hot air rises.

Doing the Experiment

1. Cut out the spiral. Poke a pencil through the hole.

2. Attach the spiral to the yardstick with the thread.

3. Hold the spiral above the heat source. (Be careful not to rest the end of the paper on the heat source.)

4. Wait and watch.

Sharing the Results

Ask, "Why does the spiral turn?" Help students understand that the hot air is rising, causing the spiral to turn. Put a second spiral in a different location. Ask, "Does it turn there? Is there moving air in the new location?" Write the locations that make the spirals turn in one list and those locations where the spirals don't turn in another. Ask, "What is alike about the 'turning' locations?"

Making Connections

Ask students to think of other evidence they have that hot air rises *(steam from a cooking pot, warm air from the heat vent)*.

Materials

- thread
- yardstick
- heat sources (radiator, light bulb, toaster)
- spiral pattern on page 177

Science Experiments for Young Learners • EMC 866

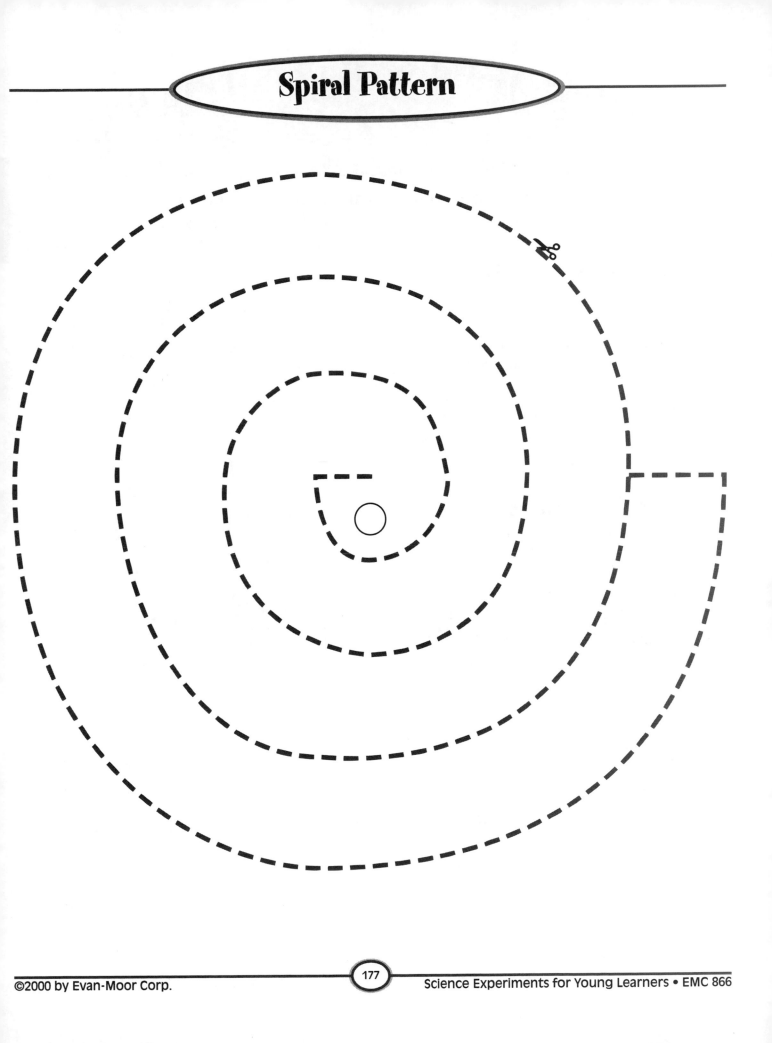

Properties of Earth Materials

Air has different physical and chemical properties.
Students observe that heated air expands and cold air contracts.

Doing the Experiment

1. Fit a balloon over the mouth of a bottle.

2. Stand the bottle in a bowl with very hot water. (Be sure students take appropriate safety precautions.)

3. Watch the balloon inflate.

4. Tip the water away. Fill the bowl with ice.

5. Observe the change. Record the results on the record sheet.

Sharing the Results

Have students describe what happened and tell why they think the change occurred.

When the air in the bottle is warmed by the hot water, the molecules move faster and farther apart. The air takes up more space, so it moves into the balloon, blowing it up. When the air is cooled by the ice, the molecules slow down and move closer together, so the balloon goes down.

Making Connections

Ask students to think about what would happen to a bunch of balloons when they are taken outdoors from a warm house on a very cold day.

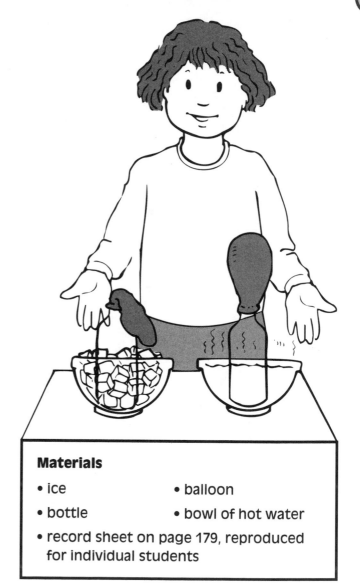

Materials

- ice
- balloon
- bottle
- bowl of hot water
- record sheet on page 179, reproduced for individual students

Name _____

Blow Up a Balloon
Without Adding Air

Draw the balloon to show what happened.

Juice Box Puffers

Properties of Earth Materials

The properties of materials make them useful.
Students experiment to discover that moving air can do work.

Doing the Experiment

1. Students hold the container so that the straw is near their cheek and squeeze the container. Ask, "What do you feel? What is coming out of the container?"

2. Put bits of paper or foam on a table.

3. Students hold the container near them and squeeze.

4. Students record what happens on their record sheets.

Sharing the Results

Ask, "What happened when you squeezed the container near the paper (or peanuts)? What moved the paper (or peanuts)?"

Air can do work.

Making Connections

Ask, "Where do you see air working around our school?" *(leaf or snow blower, blowing up balloons)*

Materials

- foam "peanuts" or bits of paper
- empty individual juice boxes with straws inside
- record sheet on page 181, reproduced for individual students

Science Experiments for Young Learners • EMC 866

Name _____

Juice Box Puffers

Draw to show what happened.

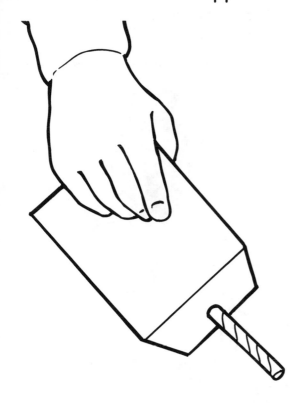

Science Experiments for Young Learners • EMC 866

Moving Air Pushes

Properties of Earth Materials

The properties of materials make them useful.
Students investigate to find out that air can do work.

Doing the Experiment

1. Make the sailboat following the directions on page 183 or purchase toy sailboats.

2. Put the boats in the water.

3. Have students try to move their boats without using their hands.

Sharing the Results

Ask, "What caused the boat to move? How is your toy boat like a real sailboat? What makes a real sailboat move?"

People have invented different ways of catching the wind and using its power to push boats along or drive machines.

Making Connections

Ask, "What are some other ways that wind can do work?"

Materials
- sailboats
- directions on page 183
- tub of water

Science Experiments for Young Learners • EMC 866

Name _____

How to Make
a Sailboat

Materials
1/2 of a small milk carton
lump of clay
tongue depressor
4″ x 4″ (10 cm) paper for sail

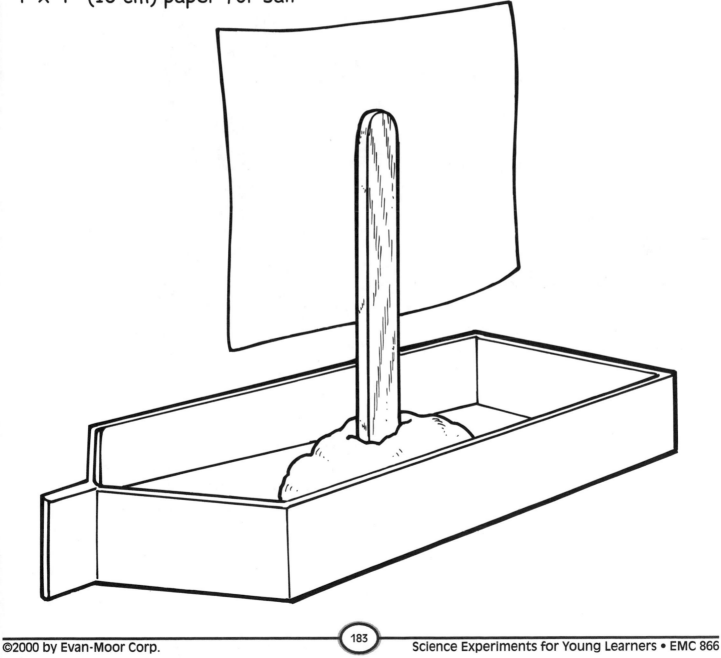

Science Experiments for Young Learners • EMC 866

Air Holds Things Up

Properties of Earth Materials

The properties of materials make them useful.

Students discover that air can hold things up.

Doing the Experiment

1. Lay a plastic bag on the table. Put a piece of paper on the bag.

2. Open another bag and catch some air.

3. Close this bag tightly.

4. Put the second bag on a table. Put a piece of paper on top of the second bag.

5. Students draw what they observe on the record sheet.

Sharing the Results

Ask, "How are the two bags different? What is holding the paper on the second bag off the table?"

Making Connections

Ask, "What other things does air hold up?" *(air inside lifeboats and lifejackets, air in cushions, air in suspension systems for cars)*

Materials

- self-closing plastic bags
- pieces of paper
- record sheet on page 185, reproduced for individual students

Science Experiments for Young Learners • EMC 866

Name ______________________________

Earth & Space
My Record Sheet
Science

Air Holds Things Up

Draw to show the bag and the paper.

Plastic Bag #1

Plastic Bag #2

What was different?

the papers　　the bags　　the air in the bags

An Air Rocket

The properties of materials make them useful.
Students discover that air pushes things.

Doing the Experiment

1. Make a launcher.
   - If the bottle cap does not have a hole in it, make one.
   - Push the narrow straw through the hole.
   - Seal the joint with modeling clay.

2. Make a rocket.
   - Cut about 4" (10 cm) off the larger straw.
   - Cut a triangle of construction paper for the tail fin.
   - Make a slit in the fin and insert the straw.
   - Put a small ball of clay in the other end—the nose of the rocket.

3. Slide the rocket over the launcher. Have students draw the rocket on their record sheets.

4. Squeeze the bottle firmly and watch the air in the bottle push the rocket into the air.

5. Have students complete the record sheet.

Sharing the Results

Students share their ideas about what made the rocket move.

When air is squashed into a small space, it is called compressed air. Compressed air has great strength and can do many different jobs.

Making Connections

Ask students if the bottle launcher reminded them of a bicycle air pump. (You push the plunger to force the air out of the pump and into the tire, and it begins to fill with air. As you keep pumping, you force in more and more air. Inside the tire, the air is squashed into a small space. The compressed air in the tire supports the bike and the rider.)

Materials
- modeling clay
- construction paper scraps
- soft plastic bottle (small sipper bottle)
- two straws (one narrower than the other)
- record sheet on page 187, reproduced for individual students

Name _____

An Air Rocket

Draw the launcher and the rocket.

At the Start	At the End

What made the rocket move?

       my hand   compressed air   an explosion

A Windwheel

Properties of Earth Materials

The properties of materials make them useful.
Students observe that wind can move things.

Doing the Experiment

1. Make a windwheel. (This step can be done by adults or older students ahead of time. Then you'll be ready for a windy day.)

   • Trace the plate onto the cardboard.

   • Cut out the circle.

   • Mark the center of the circle.

   • Draw a 2" (5 cm) square in the center of the circle.

   • Divide the square into fourths by drawing diagonal lines.

   • Cut along these lines to make four triangular flaps. (This step requires the use of a craft knife by the teacher or adult helper.)

   • Fold two opposite flaps out and the other two flaps in (back).

2. On a windy day, take the wheel outside and hold it upright on the ground. Take your hand away and watch the windwheel move.

3. Students complete the activity sheet.

Sharing the Results

Make several windwheels and have races. Try folding the flaps in different directions. Discuss which way is best.

Making Connections

Ask, "What things blow in the wind like the windwheel?" (windmills, pinwheels)

Materials

• pencil   • ruler

• scissors   • craft knife

• a large piece of thick cardboard

• a plate about 10" (25 cm) in diameter

• activity sheet on page 189, reproduced for individual students

Science Experiments for Young Learners • EMC 866

Name _____

A Windwheel

Answer the questions to show you understand.

1. It makes the wheel turn.

2. This windwheel would work best.

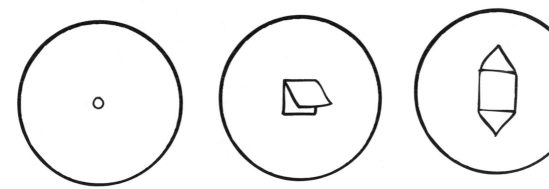

3. Moving air can move this.

 Science Experiments for Young Learners • EMC 866

Air Protects

The properties of materials make them useful.
Students observe that a layer of air can protect something.

Doing the Experiment

(You will repeat the Magic Glass experiment on page 166, with a paper towel stuffed in the bottom of the glass.)

1. Fill the bowl with water. Add food coloring.

2. Stuff a paper towel in the bottom of a clear glass.

3. Hold the glass upside down. Press it down into the water. (Make sure the glass is straight up and down.)

4. Look at the glass through the water.

5. Students record their observations on their record sheets.

Sharing the Results

Ask, "What happened to the paper towel? Why did it stay dry? What do you think would happen if the glass was tipped as it entered the water?"

Making Connections

Air protected the paper in the glass. Ask, "Can you think of another time that air protects something?" *(air bag, bubble wrap in shipping boxes)*

Materials

- water
- food coloring
- big bowl or fish tank
- record sheet on page 191, reproduced for individual students
- clear glass
- paper towel

Name _____

Air Protects

Draw the cup, paper towel, and water to show what happened.

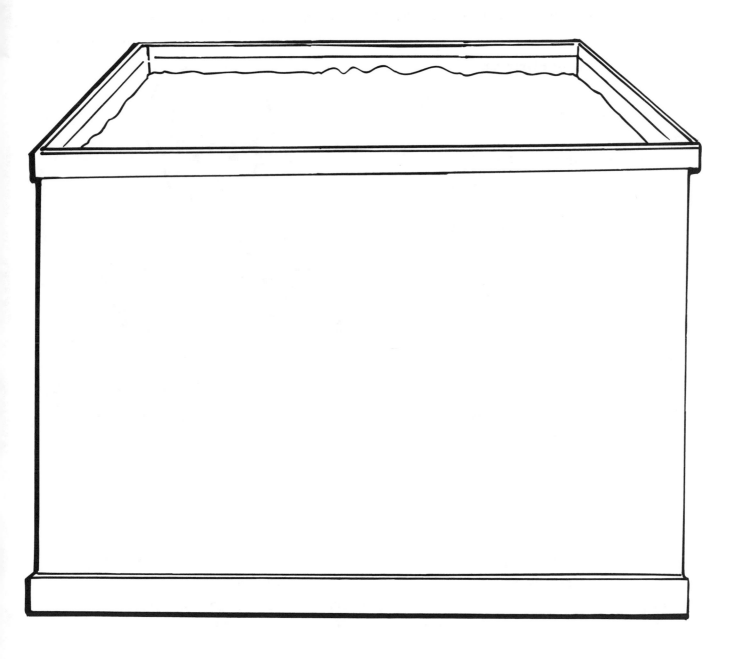

Look, No Hands!

Properties of Earth Materials

The properties of materials make them useful.
Students observe the effect of differences in air pressure.

Doing the Experiment

1. Make a hole in the bottom of a paper cup.

2. Put a sheet of paper on a table. Place the cup upside down on the paper.

3. Breathe in with your mouth over the hole and lift the cup at the same time.

4. Draw what happens on the record sheet.

Sharing the Results

After students have tried the experiment, have them share their results. Ask, "Did the paper always go up? What was different when the cup didn't lift the paper?"

When air is pulled from the cup by inhaling through the hole, the amount of air in the cup is decreased so the air pressure (or push of air) inside the cup is weak. The pressure outside the cup is much stronger. The outside air presses against the cup and holds the paper up.

Making Connections

Bring a vacuum cleaner with a wand attachment to class. Turn on the vacuum and put a piece of cardboard over the end of the wand. Ask "What happens?" Relate the cardboard staying on the wand to the paper staying on the glass. Ask, "How does the push of the air pressure make the vacuum work?"

Materials
- paper cups
- sheets of paper
- sharp pencils or scissors
- record sheet on page 193, reproduced for individual students

Science Experiments for Young Learners • EMC 866

Name _____

Look, No Hands!

Draw arrows to show how the air is pushing.

Science Experiments for Young Learners • EMC 866

Strong Paper

Properties of Earth Materials

The properties of materials make them useful.
Students observe that air pressure can be a strong force.

Doing the Experiment

1. Lay a ruler on a table so that about one-third of the ruler extends over the edge.

2. Spread the sheet of newspaper over the ruler. Make the sheet as flat as possible.

3. Hit the ruler with your hand.

Sharing the Results

Have students write a sentence on their record sheets telling what happened. Ask, "Why didn't the paper fly up?"

The air pushing down on top of the newspaper holds the paper down as you hit the ruler.

Making Connections

Compare the push of the air with the push of water. (When you swim under water you can feel the water pushing on your body. The air all around you pushes in the same way, but your body is used to it so you don't even notice.) Have students draw arrows on their record sheets to show the push of the air.

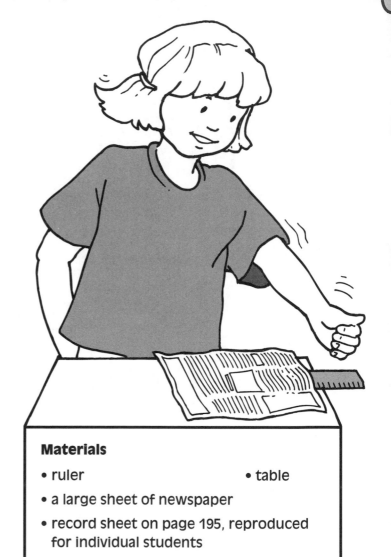

Materials
- ruler
- table
- a large sheet of newspaper
- record sheet on page 195, reproduced for individual students

Science Experiments for Young Learners • EMC 866

Name _____

Strong Paper

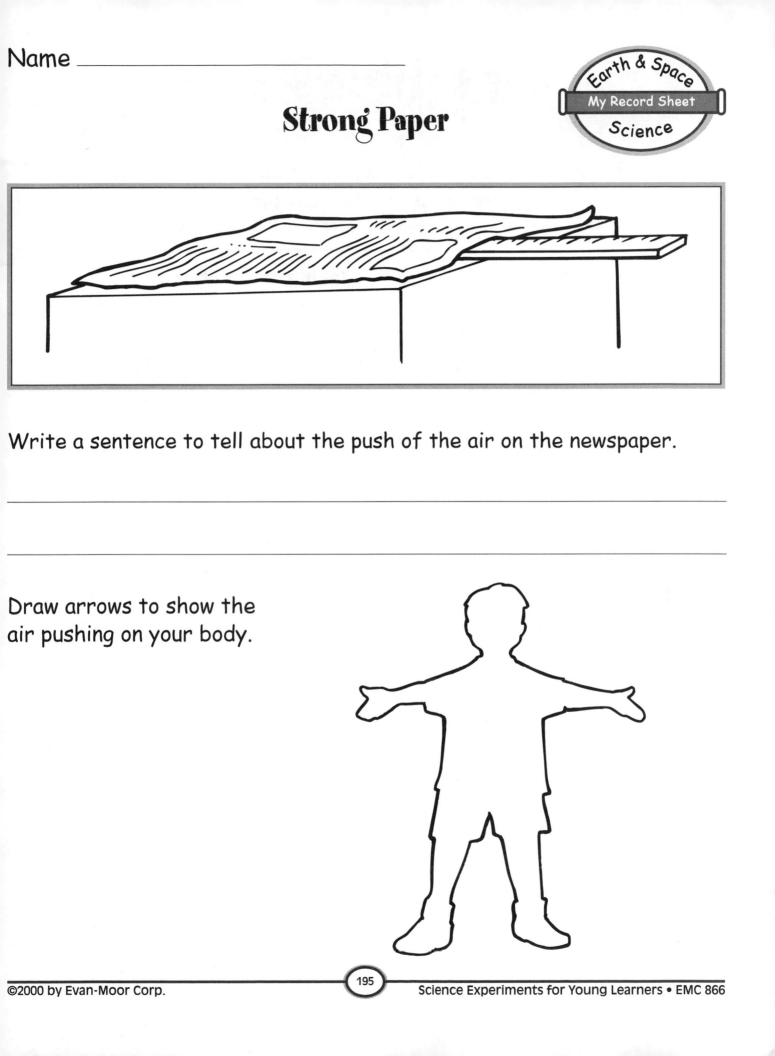

Write a sentence to tell about the push of the air on the newspaper.

_____

_____

Draw arrows to show the
air pushing on your body.

Science Experiments for Young Learners • EMC 866

Handkerchief Parachute

Properties of Earth Materials

The properties of materials make them useful.

Students discover that compressed air under a parachute makes it fall slowly.

Doing the Experiment

1. Make the handkerchief parachute.

   - Tie a piece of string to one corner of the handkerchief, thread the string through the spool, and tie it to the opposite corner of the handkerchief.

   - Tie a piece of string to one of the remaining corners, wrap the string around the spool, and tie it to the last corner of the handkerchief.

2. Hold the parachute in your hand and throw it into the air.

Sharing the Results

Ask, "Why does the handkerchief spread out and come down slowly?" Have students draw the handkerchief on the record sheet and then add arrows to show the push of the air.

The pull of gravity and the air pressing down on the parachute cause it to fall. The air under the parachute is squashed (compressed) so it has a greater pressing power than the air pressing down. This compressed air presses up inside the parachute, causing it to slow down as it falls.

Making Connections

Have students look around the classroom to find examples of air pushing in different directions.

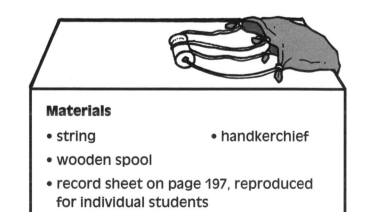

Materials
- string
- handkerchief
- wooden spool
- record sheet on page 197, reproduced for individual students

Science Experiments for Young Learners • EMC 866

Name _____

Handkerchief Parachute

Draw the handkerchief and the strings. Then draw arrows to show the pushing air.

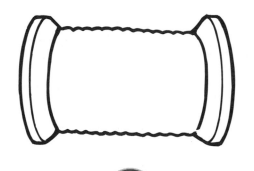

©2000 by Evan-Moor Corp.　　　　　　　　Science Experiments for Young Learners • EMC 866

Making a Rock Collection

Properties of Earth Materials

Rocks have different physical properties.

Students sort rocks by using various attributes.

Doing the Experiment

1. Distribute egg cartons.

2. Students choose rocks to put in each cup of their egg carton.

3. Have students suggest one attribute. Use the sorting mat to sort the rocks in the carton according to that attribute.

4. Repeat using different attributes:

   • size

   • hardness

   • color

   • texture

   • weight

Sharing the Results

Encourage students to share their rules for sorting as they present their collections.

Sorting by different attributes is a valuable math activity and helps students recognize that rocks can be different sizes, colors, textures, and weights.

Making Connections

Have students find additional rocks at home or on a field trip and add them to their collections.

Materials

• egg cartons (one per child)

• rocks (assorted colors and sizes)

• sorting mat on page 199, reproduced for individual students

Science Experiments for Young Learners • EMC 866

Name _____

Sorting Mat

Alike and Different

Rocks have different physical properties.
Students compare rocks by using various attributes.

Doing the Experiment

1. Put the assortment of rocks into the paper bag.

2. Each student chooses two rocks from the bag.

3. Students list on the record sheet the ways in which the two rocks are alike and the ways in which they are different (shape, color, texture, size, hardness).

Sharing the Results

Create a cumulative list of descriptors as students present their comparisons.

Making Connections

Compare the descriptors from this experiment with the sorting attributes in the previous experiment. Ask, "Can the descriptors be sorted by attribute? Are any new attributes identified?"

Materials

• a paper bag

• an assortment of rocks (two rocks per child)

• record sheet on page 201, reproduced for individual students

Science Experiments for Young Learners • EMC 866

Name _____

Alike and Different

Draw the rocks.

Rock 1	**Rock 2**

Write how the rocks are alike and how they are different.

Alike	**Different**
_____	_____
_____	_____
_____	_____
_____	_____
_____	_____

©2000 by Evan-Moor Corp.   Science Experiments for Young Learners • EMC 866

Look Closely

Properties of Earth Materials

Soil has different physical properties.

Students learn that soil is composed of many materials.

Doing the Experiment

1. Gather soil samples.

   • Record the place the sample was collected and time of the collection on the bottom of the paper plate.

   • Put one scoop of dirt on the plate.

2. Using a hand lens and pencil tip, carefully separate the dirt particles.

3. Sort like particles into different areas of the plate.

4. Think about whether any of the particles can be identified. Record findings on the record sheet.

Sharing the Results

Ask, "What kinds of materials did you find in your dirt sample? Were there any bits of rock? Were there any bits of wood? Were there any bits of bug bodies or bones? Do all the dirt samples have the same materials?" List any materials named on a class chart.

Making Connections

Have students analyze samples of dirt taken from different areas. Ask, "Do all the dirt samples have the same materials? Are the materials in a sample dependent on the place the sample is taken from?"

Materials

- hand lens
- small paper plates
- pencil
- big spoon or scoop
- several areas from which dirt can be gathered
- record sheet on page 203, reproduced for individual students

Name _____

Look Closely

After you have sorted your sample, draw to show what your plate looks like. Label each thing that you can.

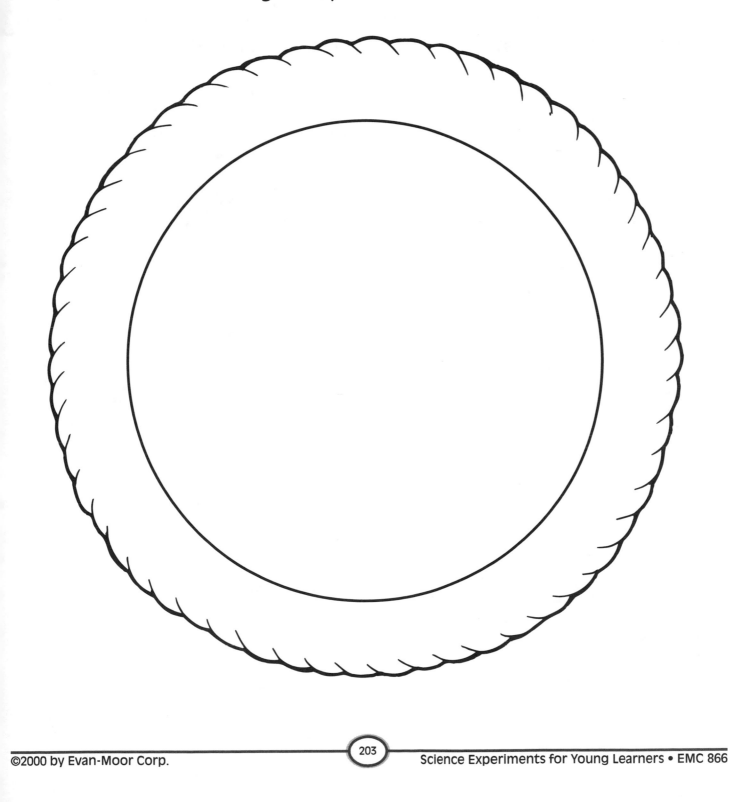

Science Experiments for Young Learners • EMC 866

Making Soil

Properties of Earth Materials

Soil has different physical properties.
Students simulate the way that soil is made.

Doing the Experiment

1. Weather the rocks. (This process is usually done by wind, rain, and ocean water over a period of a million years. You can use a hammer to speed up the process.)

   - Put a piece of sandstone in the cloth bag.

   - Put the bag on the ground.

   - Through the bag, hammer the stone until it crumbles into tiny pieces.

2. Pour the weathered rocks into the pie pan.

3. Repeat the weathering process using the dried clay. Add the crushed clay to the pie pan.

4. Add all the other dry ingredients.

5. Water the mixture in the pie pan. Use just enough water to make it moist, not soupy.

6. Stir the mixture.

7. Wait. Add water and stir every few days. Ask, "When does the mixture start looking like soil?"

Sharing the Results

As a class write a recipe for making soil. Students can copy the recipes onto their record sheets.

Making Connections

Compare your soil with soil gathered from a flowerbed. How are the two soils alike? Different? Try growing something in your new soil.

Materials

- hammer
- pie pan
- cloth bag
- goggles
- soil ingredients—piece of sandstone, piece of dried clay, dried leaves and grass, dead bugs, roots, vegetable scraps, sand, water
- record sheet on page 205, reproduced for individual students

Science Experiments for Young Learners • EMC 866

Name ______________________

A Recipe for Making Soil

Earth & Space Science — My Record Sheet

Soil

Ingredients

______________________ ______________________

______________________ ______________________

______________________ ______________________

What to Do

1. ______________________

____

2. ______________________

____

3. ______________________

____

4. ______________________

____

Comparing Soils

Properties of Earth Materials

Soils have varied abilities to support plant growth.

Students experiment to determine whether topsoil or subsoil is better for growing plants.

Doing the Experiment

1. Use the nail to punch 20 to 30 holes in the bottom of each pie pan.

2. Get permission to dig a hole. Dig about 18" deep.

3. Fill one pie pan with soil from the top of the hole. (If you are digging in a grassy area, use the soil just below the grass roots.) Label this pan "topsoil."

4. Fill the second pie pan with soil from the bottom of the hole. Label this pan "subsoil."

5. Sprinkle 1 or 2 spoonfuls of unpopped popcorn kernels on each pan of soil.

6. Set the pie pans in a shallow pan to catch drips. Water the pan gardens.

7. Set the pans in a sunny place. Water them often enough to keep them moist.

Sharing the Results

As a class, check the pans daily. Ask, "Which pan sprouted first? Which pan has the healthiest looking plants? Which soil do you think is best for growing plants?" Record the results on the record sheet.

Making Connections

Have students check with a landscaper or person working at a nursery about the best kind of soil for growing plants.

Materials

- shallow pan
- spoon
- popcorn kernels
- shovel for digging
- 2 disposable aluminum pie pans
- record sheet on page 207, reproduced for individual students
- water
- nail

Science Experiments for Young Learners • EMC 866

Name _____

Comparing Soils

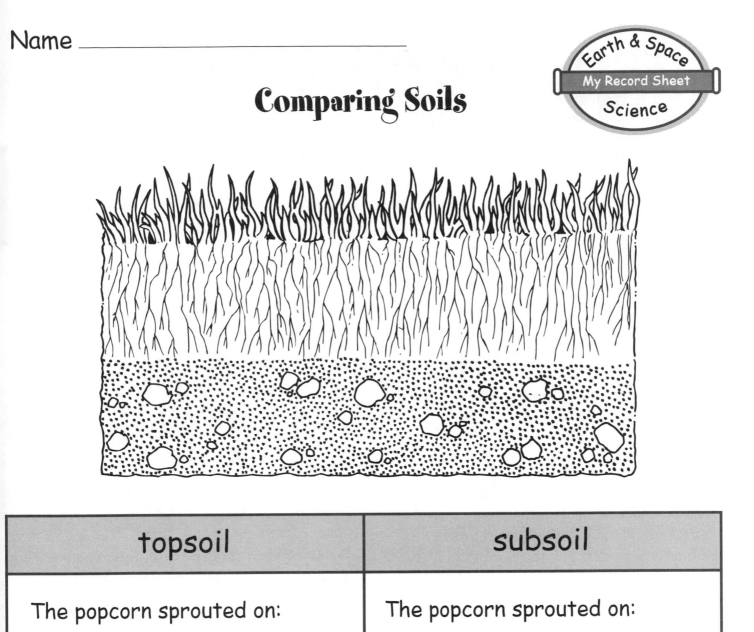

topsoil	subsoil

The popcorn sprouted on:
 	
_____
 	
The popcorn grows:
 	
  well   ok   not very well
 	
The popcorn looks:
 	
  healthy   sick   dead
	The popcorn sprouted on:
	
	_____
	
	The popcorn grows:
	
	  well ok not very well
	
	The popcorn looks:
	
	  healthy sick dead

Will It Become Soil?

Properties of Earth Materials

Earth materials have different physical properties.

Students discover that some materials are biodegradable and some are not.

Doing the Experiment

1. Fill the plastic containers with damp soil.

2. Bury each object in a container and identify it with a label.

3. Leave the containers somewhere cool and damp for a couple of weeks.

4. Dig up the objects to see if they have rotted or changed at all.

Sharing the Results

Students sort the objects into changed and unchanged piles. Complete the record sheet to reflect the findings. Ask, "Are there similarities between all the materials that decompose? Do manmade materials or natural materials seem to decompose better?"

Making Connections

Have students look at garbage at home. They may even want to bury several pieces and try the test for biodegradability. Ask, "Are some of the objects in the garbage biodegradable? What can be done with the biodegradable garbage?"

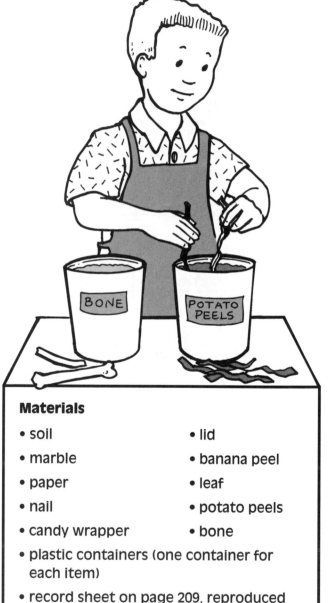

Materials

- soil
- marble
- paper
- nail
- candy wrapper
- lid
- banana peel
- leaf
- potato peels
- bone
- plastic containers (one container for each item)
- record sheet on page 209, reproduced for individual students

Science Experiments for Young Learners • EMC 866

Name _____

Will It Become Soil?

Cut and paste to show which things will become part of the soil.

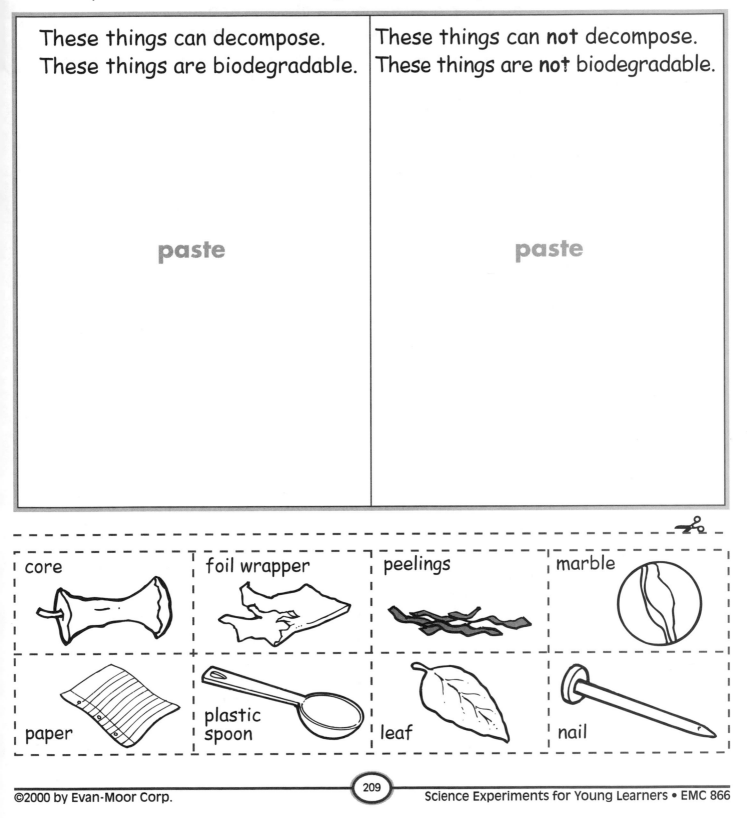

These things can decompose. These things are biodegradable.	These things can **not** decompose. These things are **not** biodegradable.
paste	paste

core

foil wrapper

peelings

marble

paper

plastic spoon

leaf

nail

Science Experiments for Young Learners • EMC 866

Making Fossils

Properties of Earth Materials

Fossils provide evidence of life long ago.
Students learn how fossils are made by making a footprint "fossil."

Doing the Experiment

1. Give each student an orange-size lump of clay and two paper towels.

2. Place the clay on one of the paper towels and press it flat to a size slightly larger than the student's foot.

3. Take off one shoe and sock. Put the clay on the floor. Step on the clay firmly and then carefully lift the foot away.

4. Using the tip of the pencil, write a name or initials to identify the print.

5. Dry or bake the clay footprint.

Sharing the Results

Ask, "How is making a footprint with clay similar to the way fossils were made? Is it easy to tell whose footprint is whose? Did the dinosaurs write their names or initials next to their footprints?"

Making Connections

If you have a class pet, make a print of its foot or place a flat piece of soft clay in its cage and let the animal walk on it. Bake the clay or let it harden.

Materials

- pencil
- paper towels
- self-hardening clay (available at craft shops) or homemade baker's clay (See recipe on page 211.)

Science Experiments for Young Learners • EMC 866

Baker's Clay Recipe

Ingredients
1 cup (288 g) of salt
1 1/2 cups (360 ml) of hot water
4 cups (500 g) of flour

1. Dissolve salt in hot water.
2. Stir in flour.
3. Knead until pliable.

Store in an airtight container. Bake at 250°F (120°C) until hard.
Baking time will depend on the size and thickness of the object.

Baker's Clay Recipe

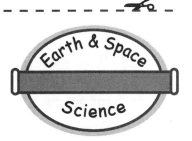

Ingredients
1 cup (288 g) of salt
1 1/2 cups (360 ml) of hot water
4 cups (500 g) of flour

1. Dissolve salt in hot water.
2. Stir in flour.
3. Knead until pliable.

Store in an airtight container. Bake at 250°F (120°C) until hard.
Baking time will depend on the size and thickness of the object.

Science Experiments for Young Learners • EMC 866

Lasting Records

Properties of Earth Materials

Fossils provide evidence of life long ago.
Students discover that a fossil looks like the thing that created it.

Doing the Experiment

1. Flatten a piece of clay to a thickness of about 1/2" (1.25 cm). Use a can or glass to cut out a circle of clay.

2. Press the key into the center of the clay until the top of the key is level with the top of the clay.

3. Carefully lift out the key.

4. Cut a strip of posterboard about 1 1/2" (4 cm) wide. Wrap this strip around the clay circle. Use paper clips to join the ends.

5. Pour plaster of Paris mix into the "mold" you have created. Fill it up to the top of the posterboard. Use a ruler to smooth off the top.

6. In about two hours you will be able to unwrap the posterboard strip and lift off the plaster cast.

Sharing the Results

Display several keys and the cast. Have students determine which key formed the cast. Ask, "How is this cast like a fossil? What can scientists learn about plants and animals by looking at fossils?"

Making Connections

Ask students to look for animal footprints in their yards. If possible, ask museum education staff or high school science teachers to share fossilized footprints with your class.

Have students complete the activity sheet, matching the objects with the casts.

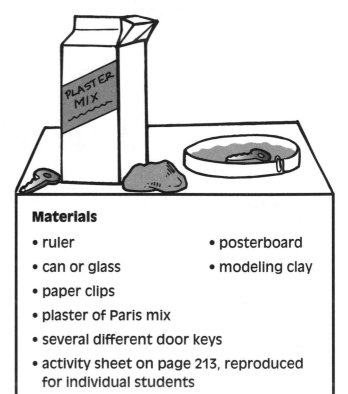

Materials

- ruler
- can or glass
- paper clips
- plaster of Paris mix
- several different door keys
- activity sheet on page 213, reproduced for individual students
- posterboard
- modeling clay

Science Experiments for Young Learners • EMC 866

Name _____

Lasting Records

Match.

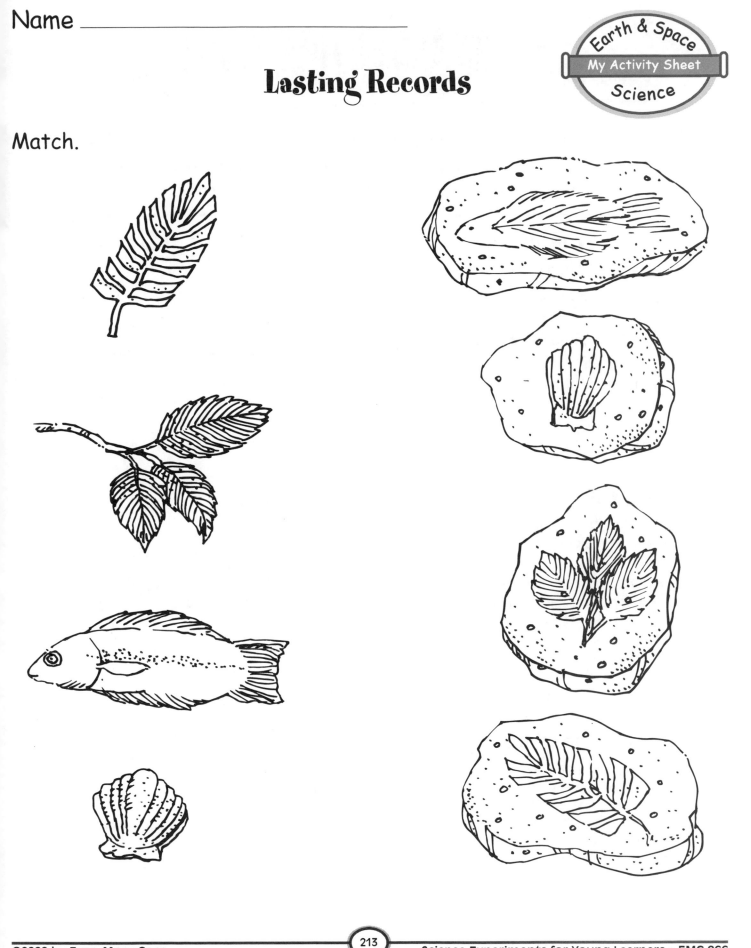

©2000 by Evan-Moor Corp.   Science Experiments for Young Learners • EMC 866

A Cloud Log

Objects in the Sky

The sun, moon, stars, and clouds have properties that can be observed.
Students draw and name the clouds they see over a period of time.

Doing the Experiment

1. Introduce the Cloud Log to students.

2. Review the types of clouds listed in the key.

3. Go to an outdoor location where you can observe clouds.

4. Draw the clouds that you see. Identify them if you can.

5. Repeat the observation experience several times.

Sharing the Results

Discuss students' logs. Make a class list of the different clouds identified.

Clouds are made up of particles of water or ice that are suspended in the air. They are formed when there is a lot of moisture in the air and it is lifted high above the earth where it cools and condenses.

Making Connections

Repeat the log experience. This time note the weather when each observation is made. Then compare the cloud formations seen with the weather. Ask, "Can the type of cloud you see help you predict the kind of weather you will have?"

Materials

- pencils
- Cloud Log on page 215, reproduced for individual students

Science Experiments for Young Learners • EMC 866

Name _____

Cloud Log

I saw these clouds.

I think they are _____.

Key:

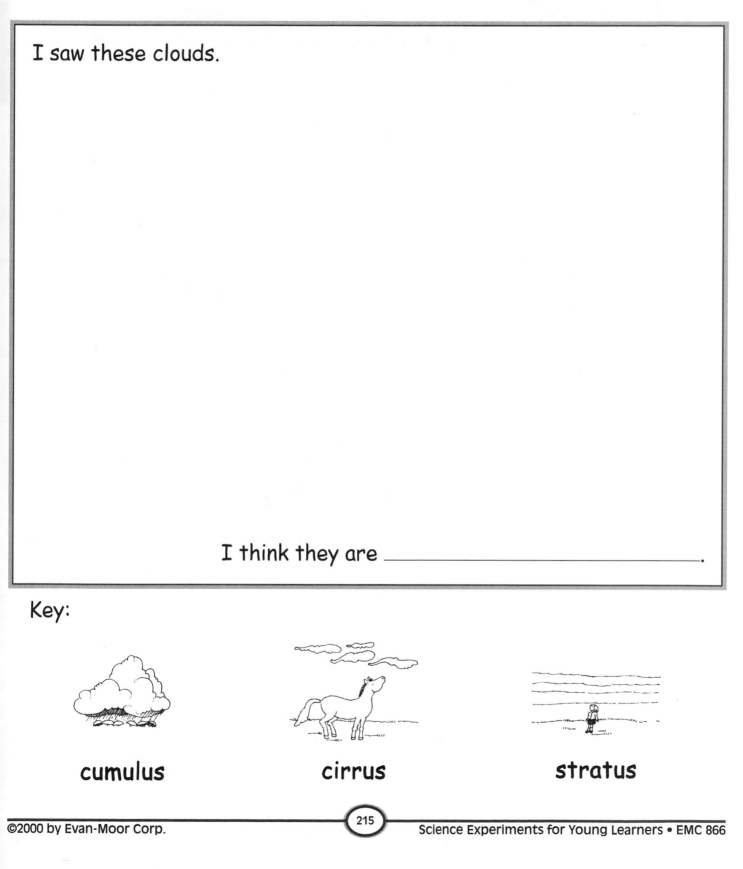

cumulus   **cirrus**   **stratus**

A Sky Alphabet

Objects in the Sky

The sun, moon, stars, and clouds have properties that can be observed.
Students create an alphabet book of objects they see in the sky.

Doing the Experiment

1. Begin this experience with an outdoor observation.

   • Spread a blanket on the ground.

   • Sit on the blanket and look at the sky. (Remind students not to look directly at the sun.)

   • List all the things that you see.

2. Alphabetize your list of objects seen in the sky.

3. Continue brainstorming until you have at least one thing for each letter of the alphabet. Remind students that there are things in the sky that can't be seen. (Air and water vapor are two examples of "invisible" things.)

Sharing the Results

Create a page for each letter of the alphabet. Have students draw and label objects they have observed.

Making Connections

Students may want to make individual alphabet books.

bird
cloud
leaf

Materials

• a blanket   • clipboard and pencil

• alphabet book page on page 217, reproduced for each letter of the alphabet

Write the letter here.

Draw what you saw in the sky.
Label your drawing.

Science Experiments for Young Learners • EMC 866

The Night Sky

Objects in the Sky

The sun, moon, stars, and clouds have properties that can be observed.
Students learn that scientists have named certain groups of stars.

Doing the Experiment

1. Make a constellation viewer.

   - Cut out one end of the shoebox.

   - Cut a circle the size of the flashlight's diameter in the opposite end.

   - Put the lid back on.

2. Using black paper, cut cards slightly larger than the open end of the box.

3. Make one constellation on each card.

   - Lay a constellation pattern on the card.

   - Punch a hole on each of the points, using a thick pin or nail.

4. Hold or tape a constellation card over the open end of the box. Place the flashlight in the box opening.

5. Close the curtains. Turn off the classroom lights. Point the box at a wall or chalkboard. Turn on the flashlight.

Sharing the Results

Explain that since ancient times, people have identified groups of stars that seem to form pictures. These star pictures are called *constellations*.

Tell students the name of each constellation. Ask, "Can you tell why the constellation might have been given this name?"

Making Connections

Visit a planetarium as a class or encourage students to look at the night sky with their families to find the constellations you have introduced.

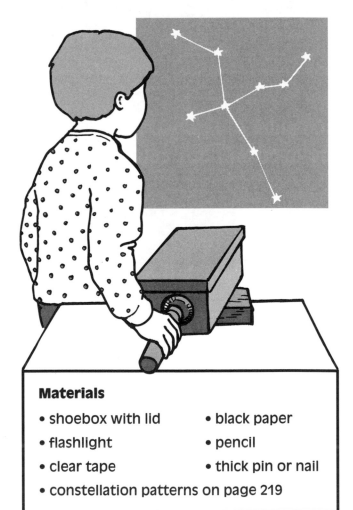

Materials
- shoebox with lid
- flashlight
- clear tape
- constellation patterns on page 219
- black paper
- pencil
- thick pin or nail

Science Experiments for Young Learners • EMC 866

Star Patterns for Familiar Constellations

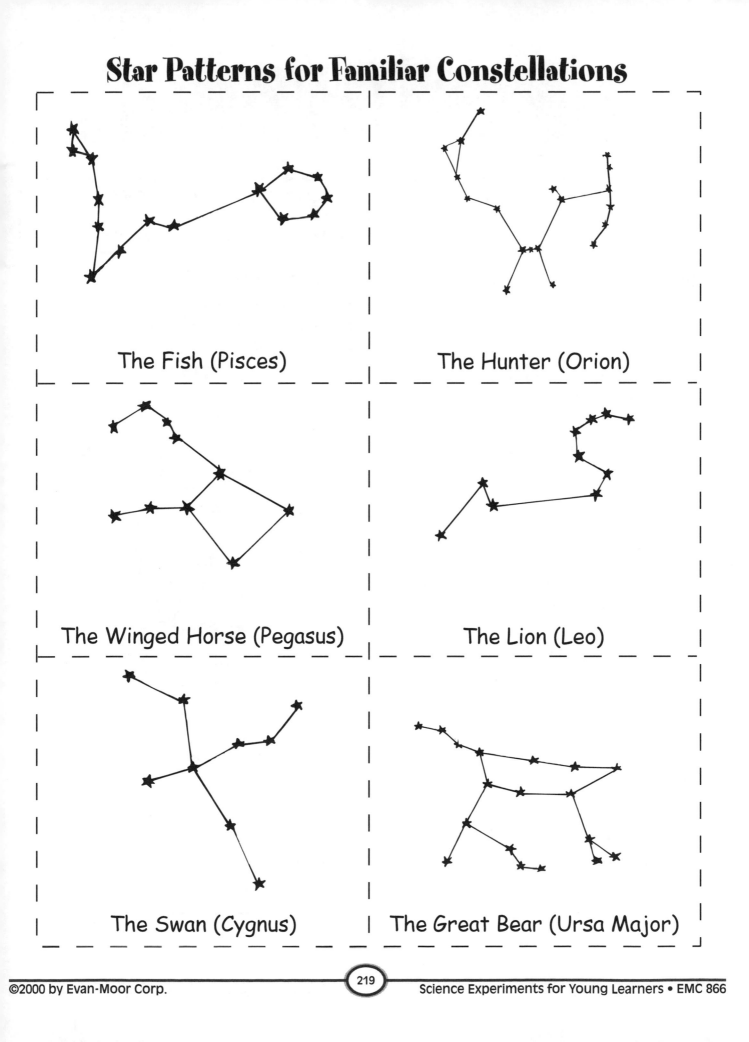

The Fish (Pisces)

The Hunter (Orion)

The Winged Horse (Pegasus)

The Lion (Leo)

The Swan (Cygnus)

The Great Bear (Ursa Major)

Science Experiments for Young Learners • EMC 866

Where Is the North Star?

Objects in the Sky

The sun, moon, stars, and clouds have properties that can be observed.
Students learn to locate the North Star.
Note: The North Star and the Big Dipper are visible only in the Northern Hemisphere.

Doing the Experiment

1. Make the North Star finder.

   - Color and cut out the North Star and the circle with the Big Dipper.

   - Attach the two pieces to the construction paper with a paper fastener.

2. Demonstrate how the circle turns and the Big Dipper constellation seems to turn around the North Star.

3. Explain that the Big Dipper in the night sky points to the North Star.

4. Suggest that students go outside at home on a clear night and find the Big Dipper. They can follow the pointer stars to locate the North Star.

Sharing the Results

Students report when they have located the North Star. Encourage them to describe the sky and the stars.

All the stars in the sky move along their own trails, but the North Star stays in the same place. This made it possible for travelers and explorers to use it to help them find their way before the invention of navigational instruments.

Making Connections

Ask, "How did the North Star help explorers? Can it help people today in the same way? How?"

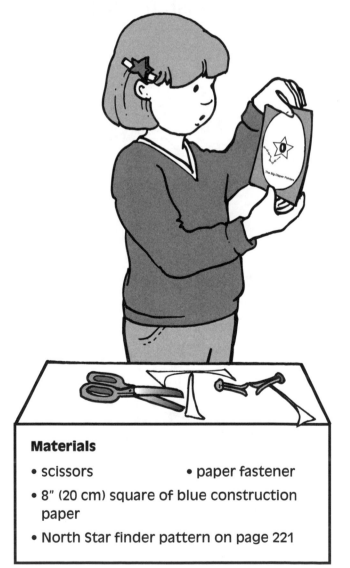

Materials

- scissors
- paper fastener
- 8" (20 cm) square of blue construction paper
- North Star finder pattern on page 221

Science Experiments for Young Learners • EMC 866

Can you find the North Star in the night sky?

The two stars at the end of the constellation called the Big Dipper always point to it.

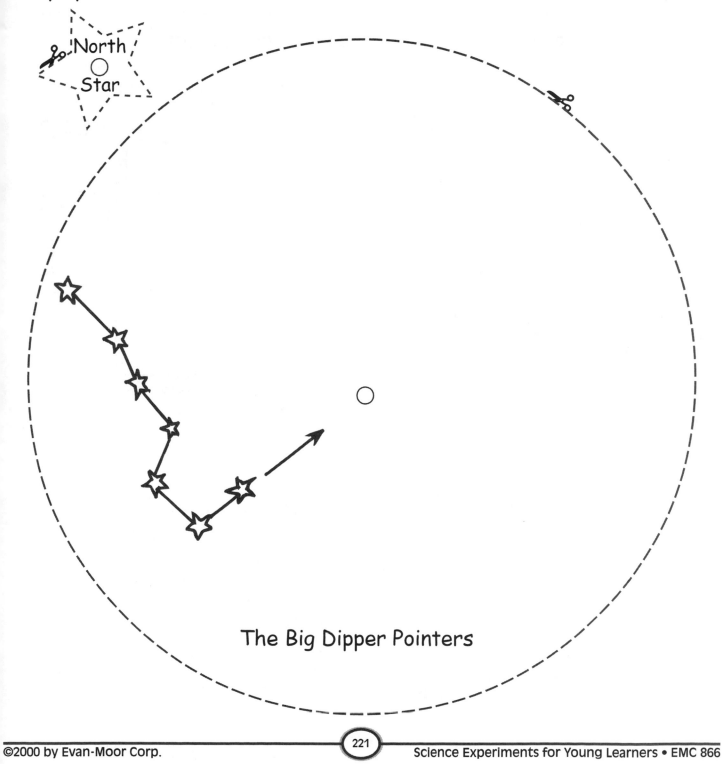

The Big Dipper Pointers

Moon Observation

Objects in the Sky

The sun, moon, stars, and clouds have properties and can be observed.
Students learn that the appearance of the moon changes.

Doing the Experiment

1. Distribute the record sheet to students.

2. Explain that this is an at-home observation. They are to go outside each evening at about the same time and look at the moon.

3. Students record their observations on the record sheet.

4. Students bring completed record sheets back to class.

Sharing the Results

Have students share their observation record sheets. Ask, "What happened during the two-week period? Did the moon look the same every night?"

While Earth revolves around the Sun, the Moon revolves around Earth. Because of the Moon's changing position, it looks different at different times. Scientists have identified the pattern of this change.

The Moon Phases

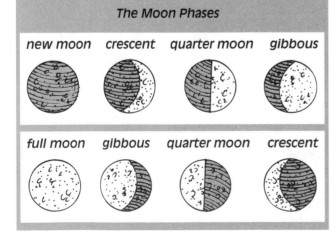

new moon · crescent · quarter moon · gibbous

full moon · gibbous · quarter moon · crescent

Making Connections

Have students continue the observation to identify each of the moon's phases.

Materials

• record sheet on page 223, reproduced for individual students

Science Experiments for Young Learners • EMC 866

Name _____

Moon Observation

Write the name of the days in the boxes.

Look at the moon each night.

Draw what it looks like in the box on that date.

Day:	Day:	Day:

Day:	Day:	Day:

Day:	Draw the shapes of the moon:

Draw the shapes of the moon:

beginning	ending

Did the shape change?   **yes   no**

The sun provides light and heat.

Students observe that the sun is a source of both light and heat.

Doing the Experiment

Note: Do both phases of this activity on a warm, sunny day.

1. Take your class on a "light" walk. (Be sure to walk both indoors and outdoors.)

   • Identify all the sources of light.

   • Record light sources on the record sheet.

2. Take your class on a "heat walk." (Be sure to walk both indoors and outdoors.)

   • Identify all the sources of heat.

   • Record heat sources on the record sheet.

Sharing the Results

Draw a large Venn diagram on the chalkboard. Label one side "light" and the other side "heat." In the appropriate places on the diagram, write all the sources of light and heat that you found on your two walks. Be sure to note that the sun is a source of both light and heat. Ask, "Are there other light and heat sources?"

Making Connections

Have students describe the benefits that result from the heat and the light we get from the sun.

It's hot on the sidewalk.

Materials

• pencils

• clipboards or portable writing surfaces

• record sheet on page 225, reproduced for individual students

Science Experiments for Young Learners • EMC 866

Name _____

Where Is It
Light and Warm?

I saw these sources of light.	I saw these sources of heat.

Science Experiments for Young Learners • EMC 866

Sun Pictures

Objects in the Sky

The sun provides light and heat.

Students observe that light energy from the sun can cause changes.

Doing the Experiment

1. Cut out several shapes (squares, triangles, free form, etc.) from the lightweight cardboard.

2. Secure each shape to the construction paper strips with a single loop of tape. (The shapes will be removed later. The tape is used to keep the shapes from shifting during the experiment.)

3. Tape the construction paper strips to a window where the sun will shine on them.

4. After a week, take down the strips and remove the shapes.

Sharing the Results

Look at the colored paper strips. Ask, "What happened? What caused the change?" Students complete their record sheets.

Making Connections

Have students think of other changes that occur as a result of light energy *(faded bulletin boards, faded displays in store windows, damage to photographs)*.

Materials

- tape
- lightweight cardboard
- 6" x 18" (15 x 45.5 cm) strips of colored construction paper, one per student
- record sheet on page 227, reproduced for individual students

Science Experiments for Young Learners • EMC 866

Name _____

Sun Pictures

At the beginning of the experiment, my colored paper was

○ a faded color

○ all one color

○ white

I put cardboard shapes on the paper. It looked like this:

At the end of a week in the sun, my colored paper was

○ a faded color

○ all one color

○ white

It looked like this:

I think that the change was caused by the

○ window glass

○ shape of the cardboard

○ light from the sun

Solar Cooking

Objects in the Sky

The sun provides light and heat.

Students observe that heat from the sun can do work.

Doing the Experiment

Note: As you are doing this experiment, be sure to caution students never to look directly into the sun or any glaring or bright spot on the solar cooker. Concentrated spots of sunlight can burn skin, so be careful with the concentrated sunlight your solar cooker gathers.

1. Line the mixing bowl with aluminum foil. Make sure that the shiny side is facing up.

2. Put your "solar cooker" in a bright, sunny spot. Try to place the cooker so that sunlight shines directly on the foil.

3. Put one marshmallow on the end of the stick.

4. Find the hot spot in your cooker. Hold your hand above the bowl. Bring it down slowly until you find the hot spot.

5. Hold the stick so that the marshmallow is in the hot spot.

Sharing the Results

Enjoy eating the roasted marshmallows. Then ask, "Can you figure out how the cooker works? Where is the hot spot?" Students record the results of their cooking on the record sheet.

Making Connections

Ask students to think about what happens to things left in direct sunlight (a piece of bread, a plant without water, a child without sunscreen).

Materials

- aluminum foil
- marshmallows
- long fork or stick
- empty mixing bowl
- record sheet on page 229, reproduced for individual students

Science Experiments for Young Learners • EMC 866

Name _____

Solar Cooking

Mark the hot spot.

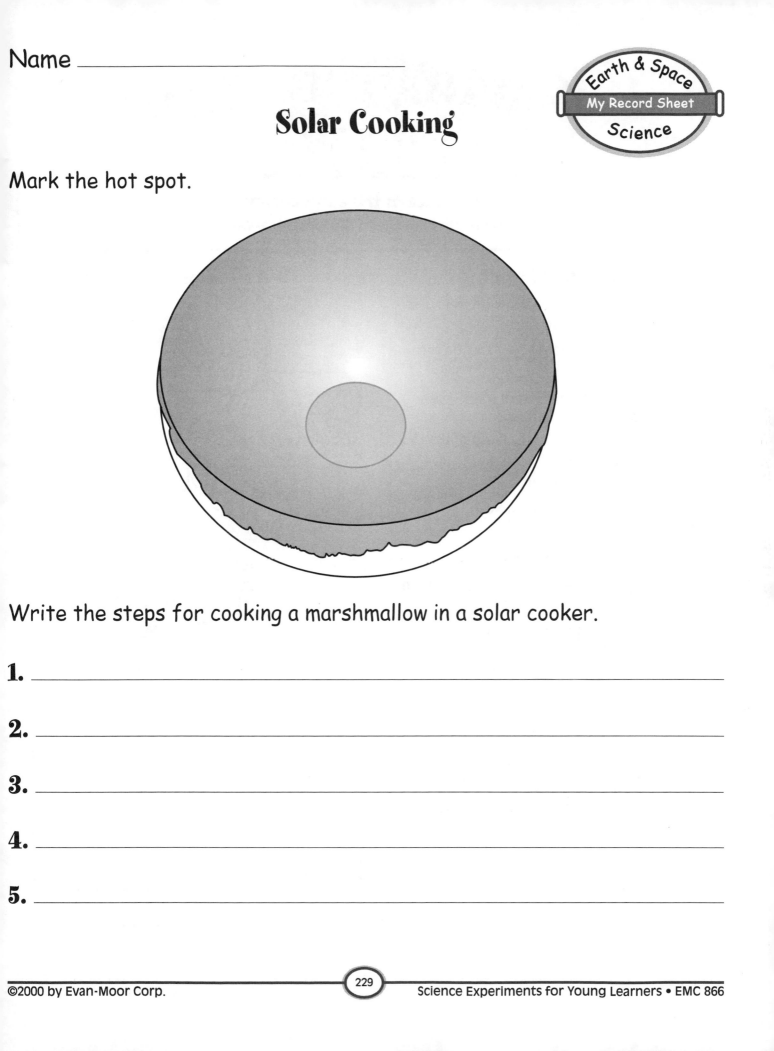

Write the steps for cooking a marshmallow in a solar cooker.

1. _____

2. _____

3. _____

4. _____

5. _____

Saving the Soil

Changes in the Earth and Sky

The surface of the earth changes.
Students experiment to understand the forces that cause soil erosion.

Doing the Experiment

Students record observations on the record sheet after each action.

1. Sprinkle several handfuls of dirt on the tray.

2. Hold the tray close to your mouth and blow on the dirt.

3. Put one end of the tray on top of the block of wood.

4. Pour water on the dirt.

5. Dump the soil in the waste can.

Sharing the Results

Discuss what students observed during the experiment. Ask, "What happened when you blew across the soil? What causes soil to blow away outdoors? What happened when you poured water on the soil? How does water wash away soil outside?"

Making Connections

Ask students to think of ways they might keep soil from being blown away or washed away. Repeat the experiment, trying as many of their suggestions as possible.

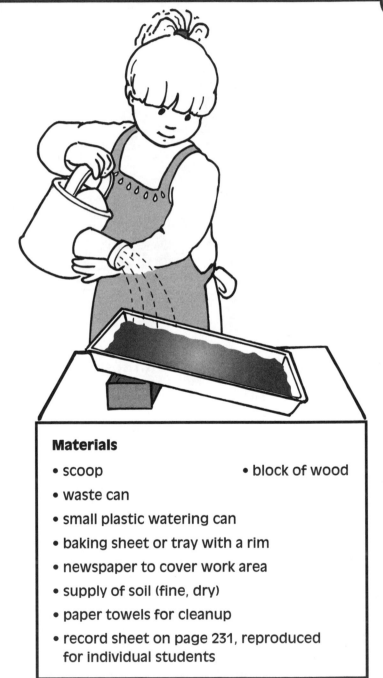

Materials

- scoop
- block of wood
- waste can
- small plastic watering can
- baking sheet or tray with a rim
- newspaper to cover work area
- supply of soil (fine, dry)
- paper towels for cleanup
- record sheet on page 231, reproduced for individual students

Science Experiments for Young Learners • EMC 866

Name _____

Saving the Soil

Circle the picture to show what happened.

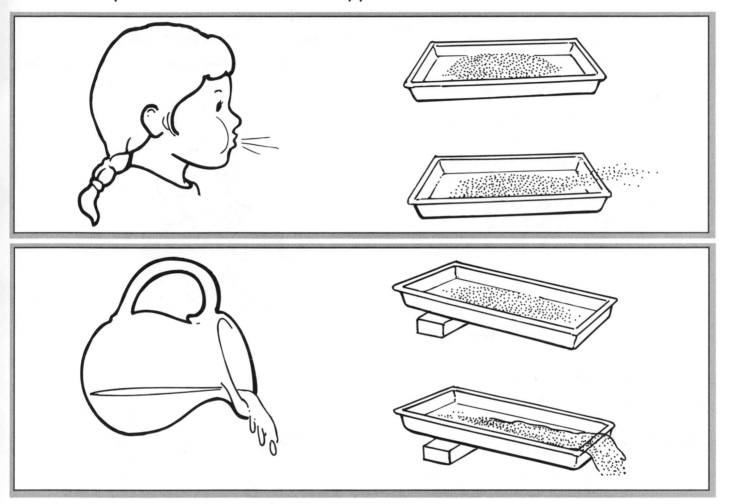

Draw a picture to show something you could do to save the soil.

Flood in the Sandbox

Changes in the Earth and Sky

The surface of the earth changes.

Students experiment to understand the changes caused by rapid processes such as floods.

Doing the Experiment

Note: This experiment may be done in the sandbox on the playground or with sand and water at the water table in the classroom.

1. Build a sand structure. It might be a castle or a tall mountain peak.

2. Draw a picture of the sand structure on the record sheet.

3. Fill the watering can with water or turn on the hose.

4. Pour or spray water on the sand structure.

5. Draw a picture to show the changes in the sand structure.

Sharing the Results

Students share their drawings and discuss the damage that the water did. Write a class description of the sand structure before and after the water "storm."

Making Connections

Ask students if any natural occurrences are like the sandbox storm. Discuss floods, heavy rainstorms, and tidal waves.

Materials
- sand
- sandbox
- hose or watering can
- record sheet on page 233, reproduced for individual students
- water

Science Experiments for Young Learners • EMC 866

Name _____

Flood in the Sandbox

This is what the sand looked like **before** the flood:

This is what the sand looked like **after** the flood:

 Science Experiments for Young Learners • EMC 866

Which Way Is It Blowing?

Changes in the Earth and Sky

Weather can be described by measurable quantities.
Students find out that wind direction can be observed.

Doing the Experiment

1. Cut an arrow from the meat tray, using the patterns on page 235.

2. Tape the arrow to one end of the straw or make a slit and slip the straw through it.

3. Put tape over the hole in one end of the spool.

4. Put the straw in the open end of the spool.

5. Secure the spool with some clay and set it outside. Watch the arrow.

Sharing the Results

Ask, "Did the arrow always point in the same direction? What made it turn?"

Making Connections

Ask, "Why is it important to know which way the wind is blowing? What people are especially concerned about which way the wind is blowing?"

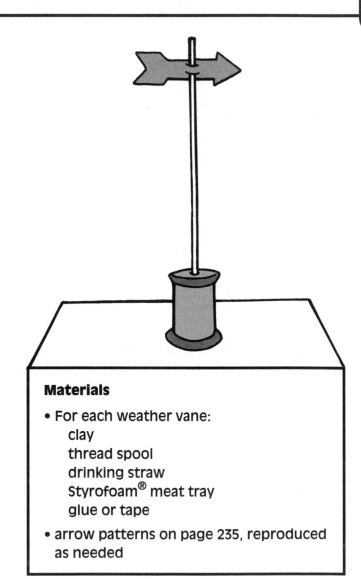

Materials

- For each weather vane:
  clay
  thread spool
  drinking straw
  Styrofoam® meat tray
  glue or tape

- arrow patterns on page 235, reproduced as needed

Science Experiments for Young Learners • EMC 866

Arrow Patterns

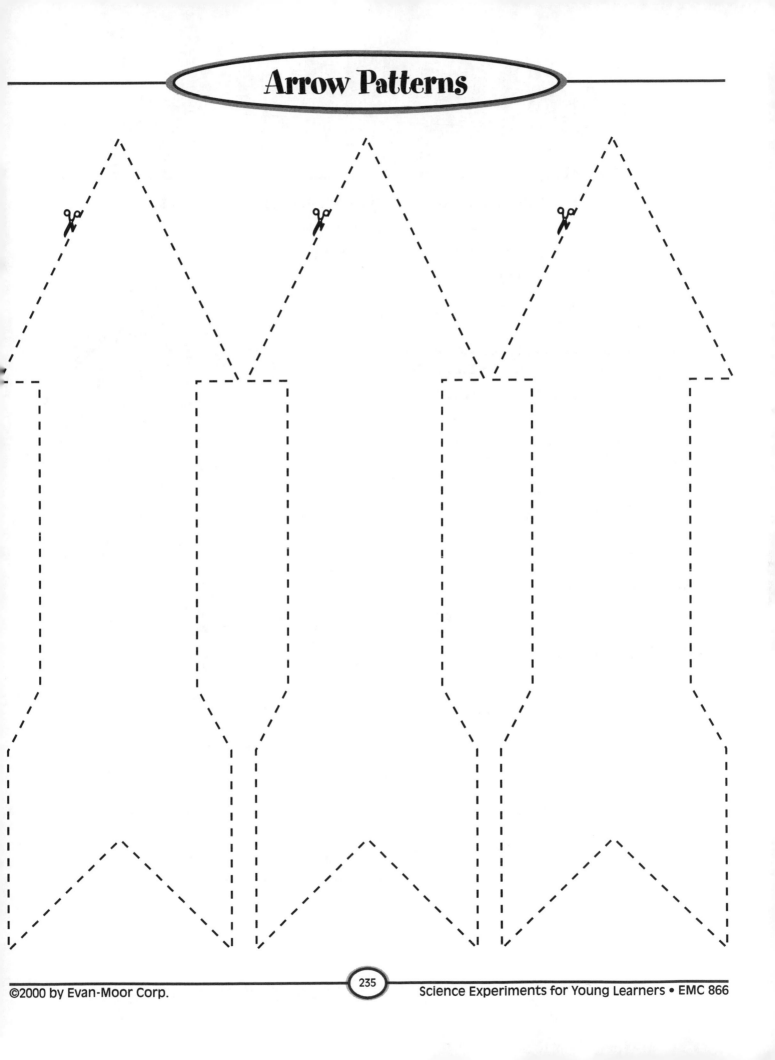

Science Experiments for Young Learners • EMC 866

A Rain Collector

Changes in the Earth and Sky

Weather can be described by measurable quantities.
Students collect and measure rainfall.

Doing the Experiment

1. Using the 2 rubber bands, strap the small ruler to the side of the bottle.

   Make sure that the bottom of the ruler is lined up with the bottom of the bottle.

2. Set the funnel in the top of the bottle.

3. Place the rain collector outside. Choose a spot where rain will be able to fall into the funnel and the collector will not be disturbed.

4. Wait until it rains. On the record sheet, record the date and the amount of rain. Empty the collector and begin again.

Sharing the Results

After a period of time, discuss your rain record. If you are able to keep the record over an extended period of time, compare different months to see which month had the most rain. Graph the results of your observations.

Making Connections

Read the weather report in your local newspaper. Note the rainfall amounts.

Note: Classroom results will not match Weather Bureau statistics exactly.

Materials
- funnel
- empty bottle
- small ruler
- 2 rubber bands
- record sheet on page 237

Name _____

How Much Rain?

Date	Rain Collected	Date	Rain Collected

Science Experiments for Young Learners • EMC 866

Daily Weather Changes

Changes in the Earth and Sky

Weather changes from day to day.
Students observe and record the weather for a month.

Doing the Experiment

1. Do a weather check. Decide which of the weather symbols best shows what the weather is like.

2. Pin the symbol on the calendar on the appropriate day.

3. Repeat the weather check daily.

Sharing the Results

Look at the completed calendar.
Ask, "How many days were sunny?
How many days were cloudy?," etc.

Making Connections

Graph the number of days in each weather category. Write statements that tell about the month's weather.

WEATHER						
SUN	MON	TUES	WED	THURS	FRI	SAT

Materials

- pins or small nails
- a standard classroom calendar form
- reproducible weather symbols on page 239

Science Experiments for Young Learners • EMC 866

Weather Symbols

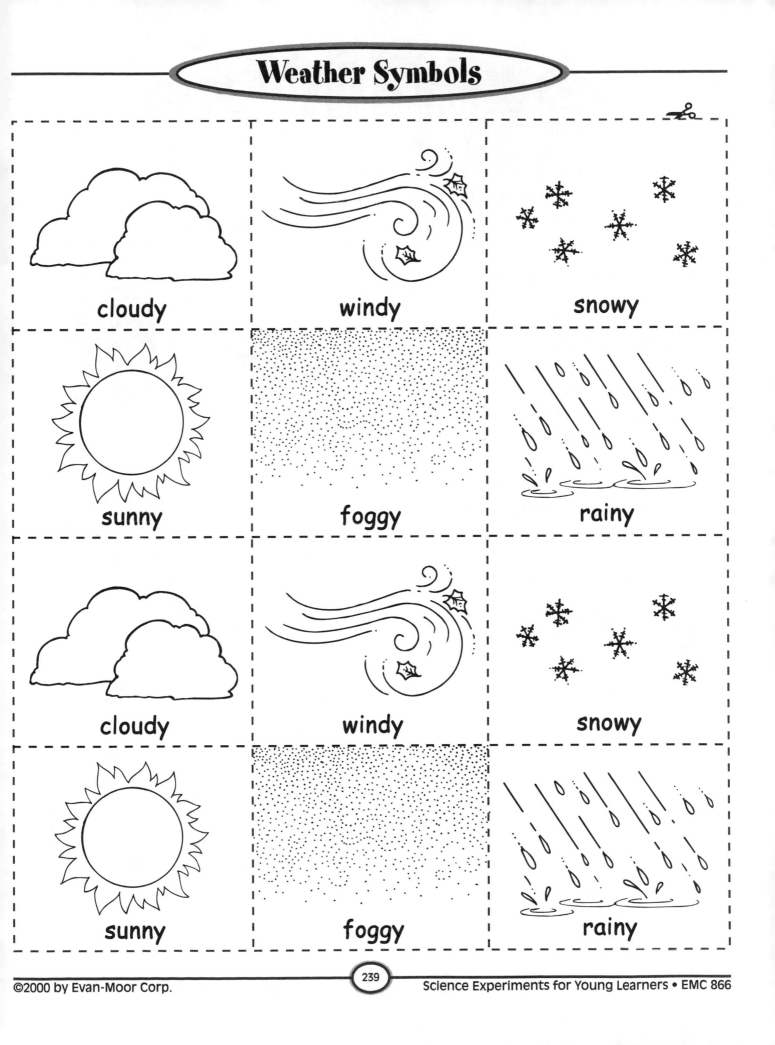

cloudy

windy

snowy

sunny

foggy

rainy

cloudy

windy

snowy

sunny

foggy

rainy

Science Experiments for Young Learners • EMC 866

Day and Night

Changes in the Earth and Sky

Objects in the sky have patterns of movement.
Students observe a demonstration that explains day and night.

Doing the Experiment

1. Make a masking tape **X** on the globe to represent your location.

2. Place the globe on a table.

3. Darken the room and shine the flashlight at the **X** on the globe.

4. Turn the globe around slowly.

5. Each time the **X** goes in or out of the light, say "day" or "night."

Sharing the Results

Ask students to explain what causes day and night. Correct any misconceptions by repeating the experiment. Have students complete the record sheet.

The rotation of the earth causes day and night.

Making Connections

Ask students to list what activities they do at night and what activities they do during the day. Ask, "Are some of the activities the same? Are some different? Are the activities determined by whether there is light?"

Materials

- globe
- masking tape
- flashlight
- darkened room
- record sheet on page 241, reproduced for individual students

Name _____

Day and Night

Draw the sun. Write "day" on the part of the earth where it is daytime. Use your pencil to shade the part of the earth where it is nighttime.

It is daytime for us when our part of the earth faces _____.

©2000 by Evan-Moor Corp.   Science Experiments for Young Learners • EMC 866

Day-Long Shadows

Changes in the Earth and Sky

Objects in the sky have patterns of movement.
Students observe a demonstration that shows the movement of the earth.

Doing the Experiment

1. Go outside on a dry, sunny morning. Find a large concrete area and mark it off as a "Do Not Enter" zone for the day.

2. Choose one person to be the shadow model.

3. Have the model stand in the center of the concrete area. With chalk, trace around the model's feet.

4. Draw around the model's shadow. Note the time and shadow length on the record sheet.

5. Three or four more times during the day, return to the same spot to draw the shadow again. Position the model in the traced footprints, trace the shadow, and note the time and shadow length.

Sharing the Results

At the end of the day, discuss the changes in the shadow tracings. Ask, "How has the shadow changed? What caused the change?"

Making Connections

Measure the length of each shadow. Graph the results. Keep the graph. Repeat the experiment during a different season. Ask, "Is the pattern of change the same? Why?"

Materials

- chalk
- a large concrete area that can be used for the whole day
- record sheet on page 243, reproduced for individual students

Science Experiments for Young Learners • EMC 866

Day-Long Shadows

The shadow model is _____ tall. (Write the height.)

The First Shadow

We traced the shadow at _____. (Write the time.)

The shadow was _____ long. (Write the length.)

The Second Shadow

We traced the shadow at _____. (Write the time.)

The shadow was _____ long. (Write the length.)

The Third Shadow

We traced the shadow at _____. (Write the time.)

The shadow was _____ long. (Write the length.)

The Fourth Shadow

We traced the shadow at _____. (Write the time.)

The shadow was _____ long. (Write the length.)

A Sundial

Changes in the Earth and Sky

Objects in the sky have patterns of movement.

Students participate in making a simple sundial.

Doing the Experiment

1. Drive the pole into a level section of cleared ground.

2. Each hour check to see where the shadow is and mark its position with a small stake.

3. Draw the shadow on the record sheet and label it with the time.

4. Check on the next sunny day to see if the pattern of shadows is the same.

Sharing the Results

Take time to discuss this important pattern of movement with your students. Many students may have the misconception that the pattern is caused by the sun moving. Use two balls to demonstrate how the earth moves around the sun.

People have been using the sun for thousands of years to keep proper time. The first sundials were made by ancient Egyptians.

Making Connections

Look around for sundials on buildings and in parks.

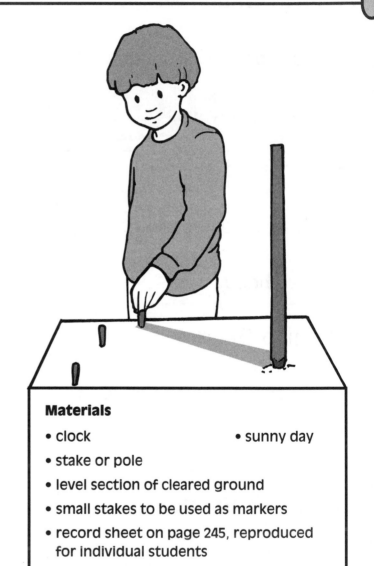

Materials

- clock
- sunny day
- stake or pole
- level section of cleared ground
- small stakes to be used as markers
- record sheet on page 245, reproduced for individual students

Science Experiments for Young Learners • EMC 866

Name _____

A Sundial

Draw the shadows. Write the times.

Name _____

_____

_____

_____

_____

_____

_____

_____

_____

_____

Science Experiments for Young Learners • EMC 866

Science and Technology

- Implement and evaluate a solution to a problem.

- Evaluate a design.

- Implement and evaluate a design.

Strong Shapes

Abilities of Technological Design

Implement and evaluate a solution to a problem.

Students use marshmallows and toothpicks to construct a "house" that will stand by itself.

Doing the Experiment

1. Give each student 20 toothpicks and 10 marshmallows.

2. Challenge them to build a house that will stand by itself.

3. Watch the building and encourage students to share techniques that are working.

4. Have students complete the record sheet to document their building.

Sharing the Results

Have students show the structures they have built. Place the completed houses on a shelf or table. Check back after a day to see which houses held their shape. Ask, "Do the strongest houses have anything in common?"

Humans have discovered that triangles are a strong shape.

Materials

- toothpicks
- marshmallows
- record sheet on page 249, reproduced for individual students

Making Connections

Give students a second chance to build with toothpicks and marshmallows. Don't limit the number of toothpicks or marshmallows, and remind students to use what they have learned about strong shapes.

Science Experiments for Young Learners • EMC 866

Name _____

Strong Shapes

My house has

_____ square shapes

_____ rectangle shapes

_____ triangle shapes

My house held its shape

well   **not so well**

Draw it here.

Set it here.

To make my house stronger I will

_____

_____

_____

_____

_____

Which Is Strongest?

Abilities of Technological Design

Evaluate a design.

Students build paper structures and determine which shapes are strongest.

Doing the Experiment

1. Punch three holes in each strip.

2. Make the following shapes using the 9" strips:

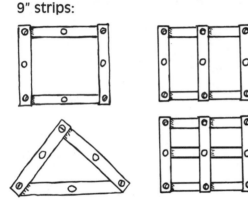

3. Test each shape by holding the bottom two corners of the shape while a student pushes against one upper corner with a finger.

4. Have students complete the record sheet.

Sharing the Results

Review the results. Ask, "Which shape was the strongest? What made it stronger?"

Making Connections

Use the 12" strips as diagonal pieces to create the following shapes. Ask, "Are they stronger than the plain squares?"

Materials

- hole punch
- paper fasteners
- old manila folders or lightweight cardboard cut into strips:
    - 18 strips, 2" x 9" (5 x 23 cm)
    - 3 strips, 2" x 12" (5 x 30.5 cm)
- record sheet on page 251, reproduced for individual students

Science Experiments for Young Learners • EMC 866

Which Is Strongest?

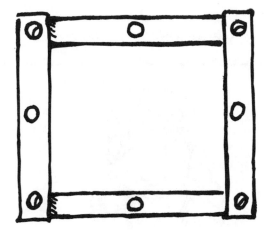

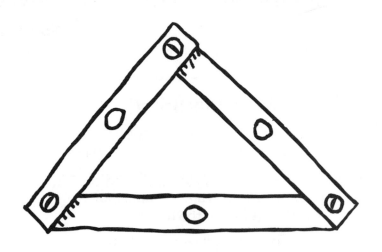

This is a strong shape.

This is not a strong shape.

This is a strong shape.

This is not a strong shape.

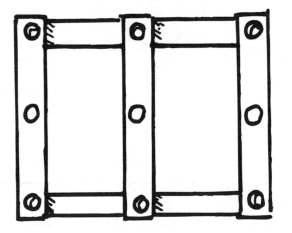

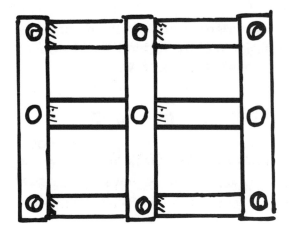

This is a strong shape.

This is not a strong shape.

This is a strong shape.

This is not a strong shape.

A Strong Wall

Abilities of Technological Design

Evaluate a design.
Students build walls and test them for strength.

Doing the Experiment

1. Build a wall with the dominoes aligned one on top of the other. Use the clay as mortar to hold the dominoes together.

2. Test the strength and durability of the wall by lifting it in the middle.

3. Build another wall with the dominoes where alternate rows are aligned.

4. Test this wall.

Sharing the Results

Have students report on the results of the experiment. Ask, "Which wall held together better?"

Have students complete the record sheet and then test their predictions by building the walls they have drawn.

Making Connections

Go on a "wall hunt" around your school and neighborhood. Note the different ways the bricks are aligned. Have students tell why they think builders chose particular arrangements.

Materials
- dominoes
- clay (for mortar)
- record sheet on page 253, reproduced for individual students

Science Experiments for Young Learners • EMC 866

Name _____

A Strong Wall

Cut out the bricks. Paste them in a pattern that would make a strong wall.

Hold Them Together!

Abilities of Technological Design

Implement and evaluate a design.
Students design a "crayon fastener."

Doing the Experiment

1. Lay out the supplies. Provide supplies in quantities so that students will have a choice.

2. Give each student three crayons.

3. Present the task—Fasten the three crayons together so you can separate them later. You may want to present the task in story form:

   "Sandy is going to the park. She is going to meet Bill there to work on a poster for school. Bill asked her to bring three crayons. How can Sandy fasten the three crayons together so she will not lose one?"

4. Challenge students to create a crayon fastener. Remind students that the fastener must allow the crayons to be separated.

   "Sandy wants to be able to use the crayons to make the poster, so she has to be able to separate them later."

5. Have students complete their record sheets to document their designs.

Sharing the Results

Have students share their fastener solutions with classmates. Have students point out what is the same about the different solutions and what is different.

Making Connections

People use fasteners to connect, hold, and stick objects together. List the fasteners found on students' clothing.

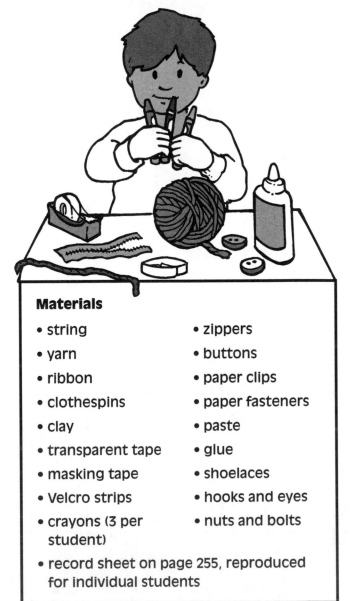

Materials

- string
- yarn
- ribbon
- clothespins
- clay
- transparent tape
- masking tape
- Velcro strips
- crayons (3 per student)
- zippers
- buttons
- paper clips
- paper fasteners
- paste
- glue
- shoelaces
- hooks and eyes
- nuts and bolts
- record sheet on page 255, reproduced for individual students

Science Experiments for Young Learners • EMC 866

Name _____

Hold Them Together!

I made my crayon fastener with:	It looked like this:

I   could   separate the crayons after I fastened them together.
      could not

My fastener could also be used for:

_____

_____

Name _____

_____

_____

_____

_____

_____

_____

_____

_____

_____

_____

Science Experiments for Young Learners • EMC 866